Mark Howard

ONE JUMP AHEAD

THE TOP NH HORSES TO FOLLOW FOR

1999/2000

THE AUTHOR
Mark Howard is 24 and graduated from Manchester University with a BA Honours Degree in History. For the last seven years, he has written the National Hunt horses to follow book *One Jump Ahead*. In addition, he has conducted a number of stable interviews for *the Racing Post Weekender* and has, recently, contributed to the *Racing Post Ten To Follow* publication, for the 1999 Flat season and 1999/2000 National Hunt season.

FRONT COVER: The brilliant DIRECT ROUTE, seen here winning his first ever novice chase at Wetherby in October 1997 in the hands of Paul Carberry, has been a tremendous horse for followers of *OJA* for the past two seasons.

Cover photograph supplied by IAN HEADINGTON. 246 Ashby Road, Hinckley, Leicestershire. LE10 1SW. Telephone: 01455 250729.

Published by MH Publications. 69, Fairgarth Drive, Kirkby Lonsdale, Carnforth, Lancashire. LA6 2FB. Telephone & Fax: 015242 71826.
E-MAIL Address: markhoward@mhpublications.freeserve.co.uk
Web site: www.mhpublications.freeserve.co.uk
(Please Note: If you are currently NOT on the M.H.Publications mailing list and you would like to be, and therefore receive all information about Future Publications, then please send or phone your name and address to the above).

Printed by STRAMONGATE PRESS. Aynam Mills, Little Aynam, Kendal, Cumbria. LA9 7AH.

All information correct at the time of going to press. Every care is taken with compilation of *One Jump Ahead*, but no responsibility is accepted by the publishers, for error or omissions or their consequences.

ISBN 0-9522127-8-1

CONTENTS

INTRODUCTION

The seventh edition of One Jump Ahead will again, hopefully, supply you with plenty of information for the 1999/2000 National Hunt season.

Once more, I have resisted the temptation to include the established stars like Istabraq and have concentrated on horses whose full potential, in my opinion, has still to be tapped. One Jump Ahead contains detailed information about a horse's preferred going, distance, type of track and time of year when it may have previously won. In short, it highlights when a horse has conditions in its favour to win.

Unlike some punters, I do back short priced horses on occasions and if you do so then OJA contains plenty of novice chasers and hurdlers who will fit this category and will raise the pulse rate one way or the other and will very often win.

OJA is also a useful guide for the Tote/Racing Post 10 to Follow competition (see Appendix) and, as illustrated on the back cover, it is possible for OJA subscribers to feature amongst the front runners.

Many readers follow the Stable Interviews very closely and, despite everyone having their favourites, I have 'rested' some and introduced some new faces such as Mark Pitman, Nicky Henderson and Champion Irish Trainer Noel Meade. With so much Irish racing being televised on The Racing Channel and in the Betting Offices, Mr Meade's comments should be extremely beneficial. As I have stated before, my advice, in general for stable interviews, is to wait for a yard to hit form and then follow the trainer's comments closely.

Mark Howard

PREFACE
by
Jimmy FitzGerald

It is now six years since I wrote the first Preface for Mark's book and each year he seems to come up with a new addition. This year he has asked fellow countryman and last season's Champion Irish Jumps trainer, Noel Meade, to conduct a stable interview.

Noel is a highly respected and very successful trainer and I look forward to keeping an eye on his horses, especially when they run in England.

As for my own stable, I have some nice three year olds which will be going jumping this season and I would also like to think I have a decent bunch of novice chasers. I have discussed my plans for this season, with Mark, later in the book.

ACKNOWLEDGEMENTS

I would like to thank all the following Trainers who have given up their time to answer my inquiries during the Summer:

Jimmy FitzGerald, Tim Easterby, Chris Grant, Nicky Henderson, Philip Hobbs, Lenny Lungo, Ferdy Murphy, Paul Nicholls, David Nicholson, Jonjo O'Neill, Mark Pitman, Mary Reveley, Noel Meade. **Plus:** James Adam, Robert Alner, Kim Bailey, Peter Beaumont, Steve Brookshaw, Terry Casey, Noel Chance, Henry Daly, David Easterby, Donald Forster, Nick Gifford, Howard Johnson, Chris Kinane, Henrietta Knight, Charlie Mann, George Moore, Hughie Morrison, Dan O'Brien, Jim Old, Amanda Perrett, Nicky Richards, Oliver Sherwood, Simon Sherwood, Sue Smith, Tom Tate, John Tuck, Paul Webber, Ian Williams, Venetia Williams.

Thank you also to Richard Pitman, Brian Gleeson, Steve Johnson and Sam McAughtry.

THE DAY OF THE SPIDER
By Sam McAughtry
IRISH FIELD Columnist

One day at the Curragh racecourse, my son-in-law, Ian Gordon, suddenly said to me: "There's a spider in your hair. Hold on, and I'll pick it out." This he did, not that it bothered me any - it's only women and poets who scream when spiders come near them - but, anyway, Ian added: "We'll have to look to see if luck comes into names of any of the runners, because spiders bring you luck."

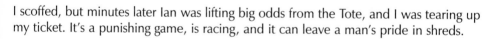

"Listen, son," I said, "don't ever throw your money away on stunts like that. This first race is for maidens and beginners. What you want to look for here is the breeding, the skill of the trainer, and whether the stable is in a winning roll these days; next, you take a look at their conformation, their appearance, their liveliness, and, finally, note the betting. I usually end up on the favourite, myself." "I know," he said, "and it's usually stuffed. I'm going for Belinda's Luck, in this one."

I scoffed, but minutes later Ian was lifting big odds from the Tote, and I was tearing up my ticket. It's a punishing game, is racing, and it can leave a man's pride in shreds.

Outside of luck like that, I don't think you can beat dedication. I haven't got it, because I get pleasure from punishing myself, like most punters, but I have noticed the number of times that young, dedicated Mark Howard gets it right without luck. Last year, his *One Jump Ahead* produced 176 winners at a strike rate of 30%.

Using my system, I might get an odd winner in the jumps this coming season, but I also have the sense, more often, to use Mark's judgement, and they'll be the ones that'll bring the sickly smile to the bookie's face. In the absence of another spider, he's the next best thing.

FOREWORD
By RICHARD PITMAN
BBC & THE RACING CHANNEL PRESENTER

Last season again proved a very successful one for *One Jump Ahead* subscribers which produced 176 winners from 596 runners at an excellent strike rate of 30%, with the Top 50 supplying 60 winners, at 32%.

OJA has been diligently written, with Mark's attention to detail a feature throughout the book. It is also refreshing that the book is not merely a list of the most obvious horses to follow but contains shrewdly judged ones which ooze potential and add to the interest.

Mark also enjoyed some success in the valuable *Tote/Racing Post* 10 To Follow competition and so it is well worth studying his selections and suggested formulations closely.

One new section for the forthcoming season is 'The Foreign Legion.' This contains horses imported from France, New Zealand and Germany. This type of horse is proving increasingly successful and these selections merit close scrutiny. The Stable Interviews provide a constant stream of winners, especially when a certain yard hits form. I will be particularly interested in the fortunes of my son Mark, who has some lovely young horses. Irish trainer Noel Meade is an astute acquisition for the book and those of you lucky enough to subscribe to *The Racing Channel* will be able to follow his horses running in Ireland.

I am sure that if you have bought *One Jump Ahead* before then you will, no doubt, agree that compared to other expensive publications, you will not find better value. I would also highly recommend Mark's interesting and profitable *Updates*, which are available throughout the season.

Richard Pitman

TYPE OF TRACK

AINTREE	National Course	Left-Handed, Galloping
	Mildmay Course	Left-Handed, Tight
ASCOT		Right-Handed, Galloping
AYR		Left-Handed, Galloping
BANGOR-ON-DEE		Left-Handed, Tight
CARLISLE		Right-Handed, Stiff / Undulating
CARTMEL		Left-Handed, Tight
CATTERICK BRIDGE		Left-Handed, Tight / Undulating
CHELTENHAM		Left-Handed, Stiff / Undulating
CHEPSTOW		Left-Handed, Stiff / Undulating
DONCASTER		Left-Handed, Galloping
EXETER		Right-Handed, Stiff / Undulating
FAKENHAM		Left-Handed, Tight / Undulating
FOLKESTONE		Right-Handed, Tight / Undulating
FONTWELL PARK	Chase Course	Figure of Eight, Tight
	Hurdle Course	Left-Handed, Tight
HAYDOCK PARK	Chase Course	Left-Handed, Galloping
	Hurdle Course	Left-Handed, Tight
HEREFORD		Right-Handed, Tight
HEXHAM		Left-Handed, Stiff / Undulating
HUNTINGDON		Right-Handed, Galloping
KELSO		Left-Handed, Tight / Undulating
KEMPTON PARK		Right-Handed, Tight
LEICESTER		Right-Handed, Stiff / Undulating
LINGFIELD PARK		Left-Handed, Tight / Undulating
LUDLOW		Right-Handed, Tight
MARKET RASEN		Right-Handed, Tight /Undulating
MUSSELBURGH		Right-Handed, Tight
NEWBURY		Left-Handed, Galloping
NEWCASTLE		Left-Handed, Galloping
NEWTON ABBOT		Left-Handed, Tight
PERTH		Right-Handed, Tight
PLUMPTON		Left-Handed, Tight /Undulating
SANDOWN PARK		Right-Handed, Galloping
SEDGEFIELD		Left-Handed, Tight / Undulating
SOUTHWELL		Left-Handed, Tight
STRATFORD-UPON-AVON		Left-Handed, Tight
TAUNTON		Right-Handed, Tight
TOWCESTER		Right-Handed, Stiff / Undulating
UTTOXETER		Left-Handed, Tight / Undulating
WARWICK		Left-Handed, Tight / Undulating
WETHERBY	Chase Course	Left-Handed, Galloping
	Hurdle Course	Left-Handed, Tight
WINCANTON		Right-Handed, Galloping
WOLVERHAMPTON		Left-Handed, Tight
WORCESTER		Left-Handed, Galloping

THE TOP 50 PROSPECTS FOR 1999/2000

ABACUS (IRE)
5 ch g Be My Native (USA) - Millers Run (Deep Run)
OWNER: Mr D.A.JOHNSON
TRAINER: M.C.PIPE. Nicholashayne, Somerset.
CAREER FORM FIGURES: 1
CAREER WIN: 1999: Feb PUNCHESTOWN Heavy NHF 2m

Many of you will be well aware that Abacus was featured in last year's edition of *One Jump Ahead* and he did not let us down by winning his sole start at the rewarding odds of 7/2. Having been trained last season by Edward O'Grady in Ireland, he begins this term in the ownership of David Johnson and training of Martin Pipe.

Abacus was always very highly regarded by O'Grady having won an Irish point at Ballacolla (Gd/Yldng) by two lengths in April 1998. Bought at the 1997 Derby Sales for Ir12,000gns, he made his debut under Rules last season in a slowly run Punchestown bumper. Making good progress with half a mile to travel, he took up the running turning for home before staying on strongly to beat Khal Dante by three and a half lengths. Edward O'Grady remarked afterwards: "He's an improving horse and had been giving me the right vibes that he was coming to himself. He will be kept for the Punchestown Festival."

Abacus never made it to Punchestown as he was subsequently bought privately by Pipe and Johnson. He looks a very exciting prospect for his new connections. Chasing will ultimately be his game but it is likely Abacus will start the season off over hurdles.

POINTS TO NOTE
Probable Best Distance   -   2 - 2½ miles
Preferred Going   -   Good / Soft
Connection's Comments: "He won a point to point and a bumper in Ireland and is a very, very nice horse who is over 17 hands. He'll make a lovely chaser next year." Owner, D.JOHNSON.

GOING:	R	W	P	TRACK:	R	W	P
Heavy	1	1	0	Right	1	1	0
				Galloping	1	1	0

TRIP:	R	W	P
2m	1	1	0

ACKZO
6 b g Ardross - Trimar Gold (Goldhill)
OWNER: Mr P.E.ATKINSON
TRAINER: F.MURPHY. West Witton, North Yorkshire.
CAREER FORM FIGURES: 3222112
CAREER WINS: 1999: Feb NEWCASTLE Gd/Sft NH 2½m; Apr CARLISLE Good NH 2½m

Ackzo was originally bought at the 1997 Tattersalls Derby Sales in Ireland by Northern owner Raymond Anderson Green for Ir50,000gns but he was found to have a wind problem and the deal fell through. However, he is now in the care of Ferdy Murphy and he looks a really good prospect for novice chases this term.

Two very promising bumper runs behind Knockara Fair and Scarlet Emperor at Wetherby and Cheltenham respectively were followed by him running the very useful Sir Bob to a neck on his hurdling debut at Newcastle in November. Ackzo did not reappear until February and he had the misfortune to come up against Splendid Melody at Catterick where he found Tom Tate's charge a neck too good, having made a mistake at the last.

However, the six year old made no mistake on his next two starts when beating Corporation Pop by nineteen lengths at Newcastle and then Choice Cut by an eased down four lengths at Carlisle's Easter meeting. Horses which have had trouble with their wind invariably prefer good ground and that is probably the case with Ackzo as he appeared to find the heavy going, on his final start, at Ayr against him. Despite that, he still ran well to finish five lengths runner up to Conchobor.

Very highly regarded by his trainer Ferdy Murphy, Ackzo is expected to make an extremely useful novice chaser this season. Two and a half miles looks his optimum trip at present.

POINTS TO NOTE
Probable Best Distance   -   2½ miles
Preferred Going   -   Good
Connection's Comments: "Built like a tank with the stamp of a chaser - he's a great prospect. He has the potential to be top class over fences." F.MURPHY

GOING:	R	W	P	TRACK:	R	W	P
Heavy	1	0	1	Left Handed	6	1	5
Soft	1	0	1	Right	1	1	0
Gd/Sft	3	1	2	Galloping	3	1	2
Good	2	1	1	Stiff/Undul.	2	1	1
				Tight	1	0	1
				Tight/Undul.	1	0	1

TRIP:	R	W	P		R	W	P
2m	2	0	2	2m 4f	3	2	1
2m 3f	1	0	1	3m	1	0	1

AGHAWADDA GOLD (IRE)

7 b g Peacock (FR) - Portane Miss (Salluceva)
OWNER: The IVY SYNDICATE
TRAINER: T.P.TATE. Tadcaster, North Yorkshire.
CAREER FORM FIGURES: 41F121 - 1117
CAREER WINS: 1998: Feb KELSO Gd/Sft NH 2m; Mar BANGOR Gd/Sft NH 2m 1f; Apr
CARLISLE Good NH 2m 1f; Nov NEWCASTLE Gd/Sft NC 2m; Dec WETHERBY Soft NC 2m:
1999: Feb NEWCASTLE Gd/Sft NC 2m

Tom Tate is looking forward to aiming his high class novice chaser from last season Aghawadda
Gold at all the major two mile handicaps this term. An ex-Irish point winner, he took very well
to fences last year winning his first three starts before running disappointingly in the Arkle Chase
at the Cheltenham Festival.

Since Cheltenham, Aghawadda Gold has undergone surgery but is reportedly in tip top shape for
the new season. Tate believes: "You can forget his run at Cheltenham as he was over the top. It
was nowhere near his true running and I am hoping he will do very well in all the big handicaps
this season." There is no mistaking the seven year old's ability as he destroyed Ballad Minstrel by
nine lengths at Wetherby's Boxing Day fixture and then Barnburgh Boy at Newcastle nearly two
months later. His biggest asset is his jumping. You would have been hard pressed to have seen a
better jumper of fences last term than him.

Aghawadda Gold practically lost any chance he had in last March's Arkle by being very slowly
away and was never able to dominate in the manner he likes to. In fact, he did well to finish
seventh behind Flagship Uberalles, in the circumstances. Many of you will remember that Tom
Tate's Ask Tom ran poorly in the Arkle Chase before going on to win the Victor Chandler Chase
the following season. There has to be a distinct possibility that Aghawadda Gold may well do the
same for his shrewd Tadcaster handler.

POINTS TO NOTE
Probable Best Distance - 2 miles
Preferred Going - Soft
Connection's Comments: "He is a stone better horse in soft ground." T.TATE

GOING:	R	W	P	TRACK:	R	W	P
Soft	1	1	0	Left Handed	9	5	1
Gd/Sft	7	4	1	Right	1	1	0
Good	2	1	0	Galloping	3	3	0
				Stiff/Undul.	2	1	0
				Tight	4	1	1
				Tight/Undul.	1	1	0

TRIP:	R	W	P		R	W	P
2m	7	4	0	2m 1f	3	2	1

ASK THE NATIVES (IRE)
5 br g Be My Native (USA) - Ask The Lady (Over The River (FR))
OWNER: Mr PAUL K.BARBER
TRAINER: P.F.NICHOLLS. Ditcheat, Somerset.
CAREER FORM FIGURES: 21
CAREER WIN: 1999: Mar WINCANTON Good NHF 2m

Ask The Natives looks a horse with a very big future, judging by his sole start for Paul Nicholls last season. An attractive looking son of Be My Native, he will really come into his own once sent chasing but there are plenty of hurdle races to be won with him before then.

Trained earlier in the season by Irish handler Liam Burke, Ask The Natives made his racecourse debut at Naas in October and displayed considerable promise to finish a staying on twelve lengths second to the above average Billywill. However, the five year old appeared to improve noticeably once under the guidance of Paul Nicholls, as he showed by winning a Wincanton bumper by a very easy five lengths in March.

Confidently ridden by Joe Tizzard, Ask The Natives made eyecatching headway on the bridle with a quarter of a mile to run. Once hitting the front, he lengthened in great style to win with tremendous authority. It is extremely rare to see a horse who is obviously built for chasing display as much speed as Ask The Natives did and on a 'speed' track such as Wincanton. Most definitely a horse to follow for both this and many years to come.

POINTS TO NOTE

Probable Best Distance	-	2½ miles	
Preferred Going	-	Good / Soft	

Connection's Comments: "He is our stamp of horse, a future chaser who is going to make a nice horse." P.NICHOLLS

GOING:	R	W	P	TRACK:	R	W	P
Yldng	1	0	1	Left Handed	1	0	1
Good	1	1	0	Right	1	1	0
				Galloping	2	1	1

TRIP:	R	W	P
2m	2	1	1

BALLINCLAY KING (IRE)
5 b g Asir - Clonroche Artic (Pauper)
OWNER: Mr J.TAQUI & Mr I.GUISE
TRAINER: F.MURPHY. West Witton, North Yorkshire.
CAREER FORM FIGURES: 14
CAREER WIN: 1999: Apr AYR Soft NHF 2m

Ballinclay King is held in the highest regard by his trainer Ferdy Murphy and it is not difficult to see why, judging by his two performances since joining the North Yorkshire based handler.

Last season, the son of Asir had displayed plenty of promise when finishing a two lengths runner-up in a four year old maiden point to point at Kill (Heavy) in Ireland. Purchased on the strength of that run by his current connections, he made his British debut in a hotly contested bumper at Ayr's Scottish Grand National meeting in April. By no means unfancied, Ballinclay King produced a superb performance as he absolutely hacked up by four lengths from the staying on Shotgun Willy. Adrian Maguire's mount barely came off the bridle.

It was therefore not at all surprising to see Ferdy Murphy pitch the five year old in at the deep end by taking on the best of the Irish bumper horses in the Paddy Power Bookmakers Champion bumper at the Punchestown Festival, eleven days later. Ridden on this occasion by the stable's top class amateur, JP McNamara, Ballinclay King moved ominously into third place rounding the final bend and, while he did not find as much as had looked likely inside the closing stages, he still ran well to be beaten just under five lengths by the home trained Our Bid.

Ballinclay King's sire Asir won the 1985 Sun Alliance Hurdle for the late Paul Kelleway, and it is very likely the same race will be in the back of Ferdy Murphy's mind for this most exciting prospect.

POINTS TO NOTE

Probable Best Distance	-	2½ miles
Preferred Going	-	Soft

Connection's Comments: "A good horse who could go right the way to the top. He's got plenty of speed." F.MURPHY

GOING:	R	W	P	TRACK:	R	W	P
Ylding	1	0	0	Left Handed	1	1	0
Soft	1	1	0	Right	1	0	0
				Galloping	2	1	0

TRIP:	R	W	P
2m	2	1	0

BARTON
6 ch g Port Etienne (FR) - Peanuts (FR) (Mistigri)
OWNER: Mr STANLEY W.CLARKE
TRAINER: T.D.EASTERBY. Great Habton, North Yorkshire.
CAREER FORM FIGURES: D2 - 1111111
CAREER WINS: 1998: Oct WETHERBY Good NH 2m 4f; WETHERBY Soft NH 2m 7f; Nov UTTOXETER Good NH 2m 4f; Dec SANDOWN Good NH 2m 6f: 1999: Jan DONCASTER Good NH 2m 4f; Mar CHELTENHAM Gd/Sft NH 2m 5f; Apr AINTREE Good NH 2m 4f

For many people, the highlight of the 1999 Cheltenham Festival was Barton's nine length victory in the Royal & Sun Alliance Hurdle, ridden by the popular Irishman Lorcan Wyer and, in doing so, providing Tim Easterby with his first Festival winner since taking over the reins from his father, Peter.

The question on everybody's lips now is to whether Barton will stay over hurdles and tackle Istabraq in the Champion Hurdle or go straight over fences, for which he would be an automatic choice for races such as the Royal & Sun Alliance Chase. From a personal point of view, it is to be hoped Barton's connections decide on the latter. There is no doubt that the six year old has the ability to win some major prizes over hurdles, particularly over two and a half miles plus and could even develop into a serious Stayers' Hurdle candidate, but should he be trained specifically with the Champion Hurdle in mind then it may prove to be a season 'wasted,' as I doubt he has the acceleration of Aidan O'Brien's dual Champion Hurdle winner.

Looking back to last season, Barton proved invincible as the ex-Charlie Brooks trained gelding won all seven of his starts. He was mightily impressive in landing the Grade 2 River Don Novices' Hurdle at Doncaster in January when beating Major Sponsor by fifteen lengths. Then, of course, came his demolition of seventeen rivals at Cheltenham. Leading two out, and still on the bridle, he powered up the hill to win unchallenged by nine lengths from Artadoin Lad. We almost certainly did not see the true Barton at Aintree, just over three weeks later, as he struggled to beat Auetaler by two lengths.

It will be fascinating to see how Barton progresses this year but when somebody such as Peter Easterby says he is the best horse to have come out of Yorkshire since Night Nurse, then you have to take notice.

POINTS TO NOTE

Probable Best Distance   -   2½ miles +
Preferred Going   -   Good

Connection's Comments: "Our latest thoughts are that we might change our minds and send him chasing next season. With a lot of horses, the later you leave the switch to fences the more difficult it becomes for them to learn." S.CLARKE

GOING:	R	W	P	TRACK:	R	W	P
Soft	1	1	0	Left Handed	7	6	1
Gd/Sft	1	1	0	Right	2	1	0
Good	7	5	1	Galloping	3	2	0
				Stiff/Undulat.	1	1	0
				Tight	4	3	1
				Tight/Undul.	1	1	0

TRIP:	R	W	P		R	W	P
2m	1	0	0	2m 5f	1	1	0
2m 1f	1	0	1	2m 6f	1	1	0
2m 4f	4	4	0	2m 7f	1	1	0

BLUE ROYAL (FR)

4 b g Dauphin du Bourg (FR) - Before The Flag (IRE) (Lomond (USA))
OWNER: Mr LYNN WILSON
TRAINER: N.J.HENDERSON. Lambourn, Berkshire.
CAREER FORM FIGURES: 211
CAREER WINS: 1999: Apr TOWCESTER Good MH 2m; PUNCHESTOWN Good NH 2m

"This is a really good horse. He's 16.2 hands and doesn't know he's been born. He's a real chaser in the making and that will be his job," remarked Nicky Henderson after Blue Royal won a valuable juvenile's event at the Punchestown Festival, by three and a half lengths from Bushman's River.

Blue Royal looks set to be the latest success story as far as French imports are concerned. The son of Dauphin du Bourg was second at Enghien (soft) over hurdles when trained by B.Barbier and also ran twice on the Flat. He began his British career by finishing an excellent short head runner-up to Norski Lad at Sandown in January and may well have prevailed but for Mick Fitzgerald dropping his whip on the run-in. However, Blue Royal made no mistake next time when landing a Towcester maiden hurdle by a very easy five lengths. He barely came off the bridle with the winning distance grossly flattering to Purple Ace who was back in second.

With the news that four and five year old novices' no longer receive quite the same allowances over fences, it is likely that Blue Royal will remain over hurdles this term. Whether he can make up into a Champion Hurdle contender remains to be seen. He has an abundance of scope with a terrific jump in him and anything he does achieve over hurdles has to be a bonus as he will make a terrific chaser one day.

POINTS TO NOTE
Probable Best Distance   -   **2 miles**
Preferred Going   -   **Good / Soft**
Connection's Comments: "You'd hope to go to Cheltenham for the next five years with this horse." Owner, LYNN WILSON.

GOING:	R	W	P	TRACK:	R	W	P
Soft	1	0	1	Right	3	2	1
Good	2	2	0	Galloping	2	1	1
				Stiff/Undul.	1	1	0

TRIP:	R	W	P
2m	3	2	1

BROTHER OF IRIS (IRE)
6 b g Decent Fellow - Granita Cafe (FR) (Arctic Tern (USA))
OWNER: M.H.G. SYSTEMS Ltd
TRAINER: Mrs G.R.REVELEY. Lingdale, Cleveland.
CAREER FORM FIGURES: 1 - 4P14 - 2111F
CAREER WINS: 1997: Mar CARLISLE Good NHF 2m 1f: 1998: Feb CARLISLE Soft NH 2½m; Nov HUNTINGDON Gd/Sft NC 2½m; Dec DONCASTER Good NC 3m: 1999: Jan DONCASTER Good NHC 3m

Mary Reveley has never been the greatest supporter of the Cheltenham Festival and that almost certainly will not have changed after last March's meeting, having watched her exciting chasing prospect Brother of Iris break his hind pastern when falling at the twelfth fence in the Royal & Sun Alliance Chase.

Thankfully, Brother of Iris has reportedly made a full recovery and will be back to contest staying handicaps this Winter. He looked a most progressive novice last term winning three of his five starts and, despite such a record, he appears very well treated for handicaps off a mark of just 119. Brother of Iris, provided his injury has no ill effects, looks a chaser capable of aspiring to a mark in the 130/140's.

Earlier in the season, he landed novices at Huntingdon and Doncaster before tackling a novices' handicap, again at Town Moor. Despite carrying eleven stone ten, the six year old looked the proverbial handicap 'snip' off a rating of 107 and so it proved. Jumping boldly, he took up the running at the fourteenth and, from then on, the race as a contest was effectively over. He eventually scored by a hard held eleven lengths.

Bearing in mind how well he had jumped previously, it was therefore a major surprise to see Brother of Iris fall at Cheltenham. Obviously, it was too far from home to say where he would have finished but he was travelling well at the time and, considering that the winner Looks Like Trouble came home a distance clear, you would like to think Brother of Iris would have rewarded each way backers. He must be followed this season and has got the Great Yorkshire Chase at Doncaster written all over him.

POINTS TO NOTE

Probable Best Distance	-	**3 miles**
Preferred Going	-	**Good**

Connection's Comments: "He has made a full recovery and will be aimed at some decent staying chases." Mrs M.REVELEY.

GOING:	R	W	P	TRACK:	R	W	P
Soft	2	1	0	Left Handed	4	2	0
Gd/Sft	3	1	0	Right	6	3	1
Good	4	3	1	Galloping	4	3	0
Gd/Fm	1	0	0	Stiff/Undul.	4	2	1
				Tight	1	0	0
				Tight/Undul.	1	0	0

TRIP:	R	W	P		R	W	P
2m	1	0	0	2m 6f	1	0	0
2m 1f	2	1	0	3m	2	2	0
2m 4f	3	2	1	3m 1f	1	0	0

CROCADEE
6 b g Rakaposhi King - Raise The Dawn (Rymer)
OWNER: KINVALE PARTNERS
TRAINER: Miss V.M.WILLIAMS. Kings Caple, Herefordshire.
CAREER FORM FIGURES: 20 - 12
CAREER WIN: 1999: Mar BANGOR Gd/Sft NHF 2m 1f

Venetia Williams enjoyed another fantastic year last season, sending out seventy four winners at a strike rate of 28%, with her win and place prize-money totalling £606,334. While hopes remain high that Teeton Mill will make a full recovery from the injury he sustained in last March's Gold Cup, the Herefordshire trainer still has plenty to look forward to, not least in the novice hurdle department. Crocadee appears to be a horse with a terrific future.

Bought out of Willie Jenks' yard at the 1998 Doncaster Spring Sales for 26,000gns, he made his debut for Miss Williams in a bumper at Bangor and won barely coming off the bridle. Leading with three furlongs to travel, he galloped his sixteen rivals into the ground and pulled eighteen lengths clear of his nearest pursuer Mini Moo Min. Understandably, Crocadee was then stepped up in grade and contested the £16,187 Grade 1 Paddy Power Bookmakers Champion bumper at the Punchestown Festival and he emerged from it with great credit. Taking up the running half a mile from home, he looked set for victory only to be collared close home by the home trained Our Bid.

The son of Rakaposhi King is improving all the time and he has the makings of a very good novice hurdler. Short term, he is likely to continue to race over the minimum trip but, judging by the way he won at Bangor, he looks a relentless galloper who will stay much further in the longer term.

POINTS TO NOTE

Probable Best Distance			-	**2 - 2½ miles**			
Preferred Going			-	**Good / Soft**			

GOING:	R	W	P	TRACK:	R	W	P
Soft	1	0	0	Left Handed	2	1	0
Gd/Sft	1	1	0	Right	2	0	2
Yldng	1	0	1	Galloping	1	0	1
Good	1	0	1	Tight	3	1	1

TRIP:	R	W	P		R	W	P
2m	3	0	2	2m 1f	1	1	0

DAWN LEADER (IRE)
8 b g Supreme Leader - Tudor Dawn (Deep Run)
OWNER: BONUSPRINT
TRAINER: J.A.B.OLD. Hackpen, Wiltshire.
CAREER FORM FIGURES: 1 - 10 - 1132 - 1213
CAREER WINS: 1996: Apr WORCESTER Gd/Fm NHF 2m: 1997: Feb SANDOWN Good NHF 2m; Dec CHELTENHAM Good NH 2m 1f: 1998: Jan HUNTINGDON Gd/Sft NH 2m; Nov NEWBURY Gd/Sft NC 2m 1f: 1999: Feb SANDOWN Good NC 2m 4f

Ever since taking charge of Dawn Leader, who was previously handled by Oliver Sherwood, Jim Old has always thought the world of this son of Supreme Leader believing him to be "the most talented horse" he has trained. Unfortunately, it looks likely that Old will lose him as George Ward plans to have his own private handler who will train his string.

A high class novice hurdler two seasons ago he made the transition to fences successfully, winning two of his four starts last term. However, just like over hurdles, he did not look an absolute natural on his first two starts but, judging by the way he won at Sandown and then finishing just over nine lengths third to Flagship Uberalles, he now looks the complete jumper. Shortly after beating Whip Hand by half a length on his chasing debut at Newbury, Old stated: "He is not going to be a great novice, but he is going to be a very good staying chaser." His latest two outings confirmed that view. Jumping soundly, he was most impressive in beating Better Offer by fifteen lengths when stepping up to two and a half miles for the first time at Sandown. Dawn Leader was then dropped back in trip for the two miles Sandeman Maghull Novices' Chase at Aintree. Once again, he jumped well but just lacked the finishing 'kick' of Flagship Uberalles but he was staying on, to suggest he will be most effective over at least two and a half miles.

Rated 135, Dawn Leader is potentially very well handicapped this season and, who knows, if he stays three miles two, he may even develop into a Cheltenham Gold Cup contender. There would be very few in the field who could match his turn of foot over such a distance.

POINTS TO NOTE

Probable Best Distance	-	**2½ miles +**
Preferred Going	-	**Good / Soft**

Connection's Comments: "He is going to be very good one day." J.OLD

GOING:	R	W	P	TRACK:	R	W	P
Gd/Sft	4	2	2	Left Handed	6	3	2
Good	6	3	2	Right	5	3	2
Gd/Fm	1	1	0	Galloping	7	5	2
				Stiff/Undul.	2	1	0
				Tight	2	0	2

TRIP:	R	W	P		R	W	P
2m	8	3	4	2m 4f	1	1	0
2m 1f	2	2	0				

DECOUPAGE
7 b g Bustino - Collage (Ela-Mana-Mou)
OWNER: Mr J.F.DEAN
TRAINER: C.R.EGERTON. Chaddleworth, Berkshire.
CAREER FORM FIGURES: 1 - 121 - 242122
CAREER WINS: 1997: Apr AYR Good NHF 2m: 1998: Jan HUNTINGDON Gd/Sft NH 2m; Apr MARKET RASEN Soft NH 2m 3f: 1999: Feb NEWBURY Good HH 2m

As readers of last season's edition of *One Jump Ahead* will know, Decoupage did us proud, after some frustratingly near-misses earlier in the year, by winning the Tote Gold Trophy at Newbury at the rewarding odds of 6/1. His victory at the Berkshire track highlight the key to Decoupage. He is a horse who must have good ground and a flat, galloping track, to show his very best form. The seven year old is again featured in *OJA*, this time as a novice chaser.

Having chased home the likes of Country Beau, Wahiba Sands and Grey Shot earlier in the year,

Decoupage had been targeted at the Newbury showpiece for some time and he won it with consumate ease as he took up the running approaching the final flight before powering three lengths clear of City Hall. Despite failing to land a substantial ante-post gamble in the County Hurdle at the Cheltenham Festival (beaten six lengths by Sir Talbot), Decoupage then ran the race of his life by getting to within three and a half lengths of the mighty Istabraq in the £66,000 Grade 1 Shell Champion Hurdle at Punchestown in April.

In many ways, Decoupage is a very similar horse to Direct Route. He possesses a tremendously high cruising speed and he loves a flat track. Bearing this in mind, while I feel sure Decoupage will be a high class novice chaser, I don't think he will ever win an Arkle Trophy as he just does not seem to like the Cheltenham hill (just like Direct Route). He has run three times at Prestbury Park and has yet to win.

POINTS TO NOTE
Probable Best Distance - **2 miles**
Preferred Going - **Good**
Connection's Comments: "If I've ever had a horse that could be a top class chaser, this is the one. I've always considered he'd be better over fences and the only reason he didn't make the switch last season was because I thought he was capable of winning the Tote Gold Trophy." C.EGERTON

GOING:	R	W	P	TRACK:	R	W	P
Soft	2	1	1	Left Handed	7	2	4
Gd/Sft	3	1	1	Right	3	2	1
Good	5	2	3	Galloping	5	3	2
				Stiff/Undul.	3	0	2
				Tight	1	0	1
				Tight/Undul.	1	1	0

TRIP:	R	W	P		R	W	P
2m	7	3	3	2m 3f	1	1	0
2m 1f	2	0	2				

DIRECT ROUTE (IRE)
8 b g Executive Perk - Mursuma (Rarity)
OWNER: Mr M.THOMPSON & Mr C.HERON
TRAINER: J.H.JOHNSON. Crook, Co.Durham.
CAREER FORM FIGURES: 1 - 11211232 - 411513P2 - 121UF11 - 2124313
CAREER WINS: 1995: May M.RASEN Gd/Fm NHF 1m 5f; Oct CARLISLE Gd/Fm NHF 2m 1f; Nov CATTERICK Gd/Fm NHF 2m: 1996: Jan MUSSELBURGH Good MH 2m; Feb KELSO Soft NHH 2¼m; Nov WETHERBY Good HH 2m; NEWCASTLE Good HH 2m: 1997: Jan KELSO Good HH 2m; Oct WETHERBY Gd/Fm NC 2m; Dec SANDOWN Good NC 2m: 1998: Apr AINTREE Good NC 2m; PUNCHESTOWN Heavy NC 2m; Dec SANDOWN Good Ch 2m: 1999: Apr AINTREE Good Ch 2½m

Taking nothing away from Call Equiname's magnificent victory in the Queen Mother Champion

Chase, the best performance by any two mile chaser last season came from Direct Route in the Grade 1 Tingle Creek Chase at Sandown in December. It made tremendous viewing, with Norman Williamson sitting on Edredon Bleu's tail all the way up the home straight before pressing the button on Direct Route after the last and going on to win by two and a half lengths.

Despite a gutsy effort to win another Grade 1 prize, the Mumm Melling Chase at Aintree, we never saw the Howard Johnson trained gelding at his best again. There are three vital ingredients for him to produce his best: a flat track, a fast run race and good ground. Given those conditions, he is the best two mile chaser in the country. Unfortunately, bearing that in mind he is never likely to win the Queen Mother Champion Chase.

Having finished third at Punchestown in April, Johnson stated: "I think he probably needs further nowadays. He won over two and a half miles at Aintree and I can see him getting three miles. He'll be stepping up in distance next season." Well, it is to be hoped that his connections have a change of heart because races such as the Tingle Creek and the Castleford Chase (a race he should have won last year) are his for the taking and he has yet to prove he really stays two and a half miles on a stiffer track than Aintree.

POINTS TO NOTE

Probable Best Distance	-	**2 miles**
Preferred Going	-	**Good**

Connection's Comments: "He loves a flat track." H.JOHNSON

GOING:	R	W	P		TRACK:	R	W	P
Heavy	1	1	0		Left Handed	18	8	7
Soft	4	1	3		Right	13	6	4
Gd/Sft	6	1	3		Galloping	12	5	4
Yldng	1	0	1		Stiff/Undul.	6	1	3
Good	15	7	4		Tight	7	4	2
Gd/Fm	4	4	0		Tight/Undul.	6	4	2

TRIP:	R	W	P			R	W	P
1m 5f	1	1	0		2m 3f	1	0	0
2m	23	10	9		2m 4f	1	1	0
2m 1f	2	1	1		2m 5f	1	0	0
2m 2f	2	1	1					

EASTON GALE
5 b g Strong Gale - Laurello (Bargello)
OWNER: Mr G.A.HUBBARD
TRAINER: G.A.HUBBARD. Woodbridge, Suffolk.
CAREER FORM FIGURES: 75252

If appearances are anything to go by then Geoff Hubbard's Easton Gale is surely a star in the making. Having seen him in the paddock at Fakenham last February, you would be hard pressed to see a better looking horse. A big rangy son of Strong Gale with tremendous scope, he is every inch a chaser in the making. He is certainly not without ability, either.

Despite still being a novice over hurdles, it is likely Easton Gale will be sent novice chasing this season. Regardless of their age, if his horses are fit and well, Geoff Hubbard is always keen to send them over fences as soon as possible.

Easton Gale had shown promise in a Cheltenham bumper, on his debut, in October. Staying on well, he finished seventh to the useful Prominent Profile. Stepping up in trip, next time, he was beaten just over nine lengths by the three times winner All Gong at Doncaster three months later. However, then came his finest performance to date. To get to within three parts of a length of the improving Count Campioni around the tight turns of Fakenham was an excellent effort. For such a big horse, the unique Norfolk track was certainly not ideal. Upped considerably in class for his penultimate start of the season, he proved no match for the likes of Barton and Auetaler in the two and a half miles novice at Aintree's Grand National meeting. The five year old then rounded off his campaign with a good three and a half lengths second to Gentle Rivage at Uttoxeter in May.

It is only a matter of time before Easton Gale breaks his duck and, the sooner he goes chasing, the sooner it will be. With Strong Promise due to return this season, Geoff Hubbard has plenty to look forward to. Easton Gale is a name we are going to hear a lot more about this year.

POINTS TO NOTE
Probable Best Distance - 2½ - 3 miles
Preferred Going - Good
Connection's Comments: "We have always thought a lot of him." C.KINANE (Assistant to G.Hubbard)

GOING:	R	W	P	TRACK:	R	W	P
Gd/Sft	2	0	1	Left Handed	5	0	2
Good	3	0	1	Galloping	1	0	0
				Stiff/Undul.	1	0	0
				Tight	1	0	0
				Tight/Undul.	2	0	2

TRIP:	R	W	P		R	W	P
2m	1	0	0	2m 6f	1	0	1
2m 4f	3	0	1				

ELTIGRI (FR)
7 b g Mistigri - Obepine II (FR) (Quart de Vin (FR))
OWNER: Mr A.T.A.WATES
TRAINER: W.T.CASEY. Beare Green, Surrey
CAREER FORM FIGURES: 4 - 031
CAREER WIN: 1999: Mar LEICESTER Soft HC 2m 7f

With 1996 Grand National winner Rough Quest now enjoying his retirement, Terry Casey has the difficult task of trying to fill the huge gap left by his former stable star. It is possible Splendid Thyne may go over fences this term but one of Casey's inmates who looked a highly progressive chaser last season was the lightly raced Eltigri.

A winner over fences at Nantes (Hvy) in November 1996, he was also placed three times over hurdles in France. Following a seasonal 'pipe opener' at Chepstow behind Rio's King last November, Eltigri stepped up on all his previous British form by getting to within thirteen lengths of the useful pair Door To Door and Russell Road at Sandown in February. However, it was over fences when he was always going to prosper and he did just that when easily landing a Leicester handicap a month later. Confidently ridden by Mick Fitzgerald, he jumped well and, having led at the second last, he pulled clear to score by eight lengths.

That was to be the last we saw of Eltigri as he injured a hind joint shortly afterwards. The good news, however, is that he is still a very unexposed chaser and, having won off a mark of just 95 at Leicester, he should still be one step ahead of the handicapper. Three miles looks like being his optimum trip and there are definitely more races to be won with this improving chaser.

POINTS TO NOTE
Probable Best Distance - **3 miles**
Preferred Going - **Soft**
Connection's Comments: "He is a horse I like a lot and he should be back on the track by November." T.CASEY

GOING:	R	W	P	TRACK:	R	W	P
Soft	1	1	0	Left Handed	1	0	0
Gd/Sft	2	0	1	Right	3	1	1
Good	1	0	0	Galloping	1	0	1
				Stiff/Undul.	3	1	0

TRIP:	R	W	P		R	W	P
2m 4f	1	0	0	2m 7f	1	1	0
2m 6f	1	0	1	3m	1	0	0

ERRAND BOY
5 b g Ardross - Love Match (USA) (Affiliate (USA))
OWNER: Mr TREVOR HEMMINGS
TRAINER: Mrs S.J.SMITH. High Eldwick, West Yorkshire.
CAREER FORM FIGURES: 12
CAREER WIN: 1999: Mar CATTERICK Soft NHF 2m

Errand Boy's debut was always going to be of great interest, having been bought at the 1998 Doncaster Spring Sales for 50,000gns. He was originally in training with Micky Hammond but, by the time he reached a racecourse, he was under the guidance of Sue and Harvey Smith.

He made an instant impression when winning a Catterick bumper by three and a half lengths from dual winner Ireland's Eye. Never far off the leaders, Errand Boy was given a super ride by

Seamus Durack as he stuck to the inside up the home straight where the ground was undoubtedly fresher. He always looked in command as he held John Norton's runner comfortably.

His connections were obviously impressed as the five year old was allowed to take his chance in the Grade 2 Champion bumper at Aintree on National day, and he certainly did not disgrace himself. In fact, he ran a splendid race to finish four lengths second to King of the Castle. He was staying on all the time having got outpaced at the half mile marker. His run at Aintree illustrated the point that Errand Boy will be even more effective over two and a half miles. The fact he is also a half brother to the former smart stayer Burgoyne confirms that view.

The owner / trainer combination of Trevor Hemmings and Sue Smith did very well in novice hurdles with Tonoco last season and, while Errand Boy does not possess his stablemate's pace, they are likely to do the same this term with this most promising son of Ardross.

POINTS TO NOTE

| Probable Best Distance | - | 2½ miles + |
| Preferred Going | - | Good / Soft |

GOING:	R	W	P		TRACK:	R	W	P
Soft	1	1	0		Left Handed	2	1	1
Good	1	0	1		Tight	1	0	1
					Tight/Undul.	1	1	0

TRIP:	R	W	P
2m	2	1	1

EVER BLESSED (IRE)
7 b g Lafontaine (USA) - Sanctify (Joshua)
OWNER: The EVER BLESSED PARTNERSHIP
TRAINER: M.A.PITMAN. Upper Lambourn, Berkshire.
CAREER FORM FIGURES: 12 - 3 - 232 - 2111F
CAREER WINS: 1996: Feb ASCOT Soft NHF 2m: 1999: Jan LEICESTER Soft MC 2m 7f; Mar TOWCESTER Soft NC 2m 6f; BANGOR Soft NC 3m

As everyone knows, Mark Pitman will be particularly strong in the novice hurdle department this term but he has also inherited some super chasers from his mother Jenny, not least the progressive Ever Blessed. Mrs Pitman maintained throughout his career that Ever Blessed would make a high class chaser and, bearing in mind he starts this season off a mark of just 119, then he is most definitely a horse to follow.

Following a less than spectacular chasing debut at Newbury (2½ miles) behind No Retreat, the seven year old improved dramatically when stepped up in distance. He beat the useful King's Banker by a neck at Leicester, Coulin Loch by a distance at Towcester and was then left clear at the third last at Bangor when Jocks Cross fell. As a result, Ever Blessed was allowed to take his chance in the Grade 2 Mumm Mildmay Novices' Chase at Aintree. He appeared to be travelling like a winner when he fell at the sixth which allowed Spendid to score comfortably. There was much debate at the time but I feel if Ever Blessed had stood up then he would have prevailed, particularly as he was three to four lengths clear of the ridden along Spendid.

Stamina is, without doubt, Ever Blessed's strong suit and it is not difficult to see him contesting some of the top staying handicap chases such as the Welsh National. Given his favoured soft ground, he will be a major player.

POINTS TO NOTE

Probable Best Distance	-	3 miles +
Preferred Going	-	Soft

Connection's Comments: "Ever Blessed has got plenty of scope and the penny is starting to drop with him. He needs three miles and is a horse to follow this season." Mrs J.PITMAN OBE

GOING:	R	W	P		TRACK:	R	W	P
Heavy	1	0	1		Left Handed	6	1	4
Soft	6	4	2		Right	5	3	2
Gd/Sft	1	0	1		Galloping	5	1	4
Good	3	0	2		Stiff/Undul.	3	2	1
					Tight	3	1	1

TRIP:	R	W	P			R	W	P
2m	2	1	1		2m 7f	1	1	0
2m 1f	1	0	1		3m	1	1	0
2m 4f	3	0	3		3m 1f	1	0	0
2m 6f	2	1	1					

FADALKO (FR)
6 b g Cadoudal (FR) - Kalliste (FR) (Calicot (FR))
OWNER: Mr ROBERT OGDEN CBE
TRAINER: P.F.NICHOLLS. Ditcheat, Somerset.
CAREER FORM FIGURES: (Excludes French form) 25P6210
CAREER WIN: 1999: Apr AYR Soft HH 2m

"Anything that happens this season is a bonus as far as we are concerned as this horse is very much one to look forward to in novice chases next year," remarked Paul Nicholls last season about the very exciting ex-French trained Fadalko. A winner of three of his four starts in his native France (all in very soft ground at Auteuil), Fadalko already looks a leading contender for the Arkle Chase at Cheltenham.

On arriving in Britain, the Robert Ogden owned gelding was tried over two and a half miles or further but appeared not to stay. Once dropped back to the minimum trip, he looked a completely different horse and it resulted in a three quarters of a length victory over Potentate in the Scottish Champion Hurdle at Ayr. It was a fine achievement, especially as Fadalko had only been beaten a length by Kinnescash in a competitive Aintree handicap just a week earlier. He was probably over the top by the time he came home last of the twenty one finishers in the Swinton Handicap Hurdle at Haydock in May. However, to reach a hurdles rating of 143 by the end of the season was an excellent effort.

A big strong gelding, Fadalko is a chaser in the making in every respect and there must be every chance that he can follow in the footsteps of stablemate Flagship Uberalles and develop into a major contender for all the top two mile novice chases this season.

POINTS TO NOTE
Probable Best Distance — 2 miles
Preferred Going — Soft
Connection's Comments: "He took time to acclimatise when he first came over from France but he really bloomed through the Spring. I can hardly wait to get him chasing next Autumn. He's already jumped fences well at home and could be our Arkle horse for this season." P.NICHOLLS

GOING:	R	W	P	TRACK:	R	W	P
Heavy	1	0	0	Left Handed	6	1	2
Soft	2	1	0	Right	1	0	0
Gd/Sft	2	0	1	Galloping	1	1	0
Good	2	0	1	Stiff/Undul.	1	0	0
				Tight	5	0	2

TRIP:	R	W	P		R	W	P
2m	3	1	1	2m 5f	2	0	0
2m 4f	1	0	1	2m 6f	1	0	0

FRENCHMAN'S CREEK
5 b g Emperor Fountain - Hollow Creek (Tarqogan)
OWNER: Mr H.MORRISON
TRAINER: H.MORRISON. East Ilsley, Berkshire.
CAREER FORM FIGURES: 3

Hughie Morrison had just seven runners during the last National Hunt season with his two winners coming from his juvenile hurdler Tom Paddington. Unfortunately, he broke down badly at Newbury last term and is expected to miss this season. His flag bearer for this year is likely to be his highly promising bumper horse Frenchman's Creek.

Frenchman's Creek made his racecourse debut in arguably the most competitive bumper, outside the Cheltenham Festival, run all season. His opening price of 20/1 was clipped to 16's by the time the tapes went up and he ran a smashing race, brimful of promise for the future. Tom Jenks' mount made his effort with two furlongs to run and, while he never really got on terms with the winner Golden Alpha, he stayed on strongly to claim third place. The most interesting aspect of the race was the fact that back in fourth, six lengths behind Frenchman's Creek, was the subsequent Cheltenham Festival bumper winner Monsignor. Admittedly, Mark Pitman stated that the slow early pace had brought about the downfall of his charge but just the fact Hughie

Morrison's gelding beat him, on his racecourse debut, is an excellent effort.

Frenchman's Creek possesses tremendous scope and he will one day make a high class chaser but he is sure to win more than his share of hurdles races beforehand. Most definitely one to follow.

POINTS TO NOTE

Probable Best Distance	-	**2 - 2½ miles**
Preferred Going	-	**Good / Soft**

Connection's Comments: "He is a horse with a serious engine." H.MORRISON

GOING:	R	W	P	TRACK:	R	W	P
Good	1	0	1	Left Handed	1	0	1
				Galloping	1	0	1

TRIP:	R	W	P
2m	1	0	1

GOOD HEART (IRE)
4 ch g Be My Native (USA) - Johnstown Love (IRE) (Golden Love)
OWNER: Mrs SYLVIA CLEGG
TRAINER: T.P.TATE. Tadcaster, North Yorkshire.
CAREER FORM FIGURES: 1
CAREER WIN: 1999: Feb HAYDOCK Soft NHF 2m

One of the most impressive winning bumper performances of last season came from the Tom Tate trained Good Heart at Haydock in February. Carrying just ten stone one under the guidance of Liam Cooper, Good Heart blitzed his fifteen rivals by upwards of eleven lengths.

Not totally unfancied at 12/1, the son of Be My Native was always moving well for Cooper and took up the running with three furlongs to run. Understandably, he still looked quite green in the closing stages and, bearing in mind the ground was riding very testing, it was a splendid start to his career. Good Heart raced in his trainer's colours but he has, significantly, been bought since by one of Tom Tate's most well known and loyal patrons, Mrs Sylvia Clegg, whose colours were made famous by Tate's star chaser Lo Stregone.

Still only four, Good Heart has a most promising future in front of him. He will doubtless go on and make a very good chaser one day but before then he will win plenty of hurdle races.

POINTS TO NOTE

Probable Best Distance	-	**2 - 2½ miles**
Preferred Going	-	**Good / Soft**

Connection's Comments: "We are expecting him to make up into a very decent novice hurdler this season." JAMES TATE

GOING:	R	W	P		TRACK:	R	W	P
Soft	1	1	0		Left Handed	1	1	0
					Tight	1	1	0

TRIP:	R	W	P
2m	1	1	0

GOODTIME GEORGE (IRE)

6 b g Strong Gale - Game Sunset (Menelek)
OWNER: Mrs M.J.BONE
TRAINER: M.A.PITMAN. Upper Lambourn, Berkshire.
CAREER FORM FIGURES: 32557 - 2211013
CAREER WINS: 1998: Dec STRATFORD Soft MH 2¾m: 1999: Jan DONCASTER Good NH
3m; May UTTOXETER Gd/Fm NH 3m

Goodtime George is a lovely prospect for novice chases this season. He has been nurtured through his hurdling career by Jenny Pitman and her son Mark looks set to reap the benefits this season.

A strong chasing type, Goodtime George took time to finally get off the mark over hurdles but when it did come at Stratford in December, he did so in some style. Jumping superbly, he pulverised his ten rivals including Percy Parkeeper by upwards of twenty nine lengths. He followed that up with another impressive performance when accounting for Supreme Day by nine lengths at Doncaster a month later. While the son of Strong Gale never landed a telling blow in the Royal & Sun Alliance Hurdle at Cheltenham behind Barton, he did record another very easy success at Uttoxeter in May. Leading at the third last, he was never in the slightest danger as he cruised home by two and a half lengths from Northday. Having been on the go since October, Goodtime George had probably had enough by the time he was only third, again at the Staffordshire track, behind Latchford towards the end of May.

Goodtime George earned a handicap rating of 130 over hurdles, which is a fine achievement considering he is very much a chaser in the making and he is likely to surpass that mark once sent chasing. Despite his win at Stratford in soft ground, Goodtime George is a far better horse given good ground.

POINTS TO NOTE
Probable Best Distance   -   3 miles
Preferred Going   -   Good
Connection's Comments: "This is a chaser and it's the next two years at Cheltenham that are important to me." Mrs J.PITMAN OBE

GOING:	R	W	P		TRACK:	R	W	P
Soft	2	1	0		Left Handed	10	3	3
Gd/Sft	2	0	0		Right	2	0	2
Good	6	1	4		Galloping	5	1	2
Gd/Fm	2	1	1		Stiff/Undul.	3	0	2

| | | | Tight | 2 | 1 | 0 |
| | | | Tight/Undul. | 2 | 1 | 1 |

TRIP:	R	W	P		R	W	P
2m	3	0	1	2m 6f	3	1	1
2m 1f	1	0	1	3m	3	2	1
2m 5f	2	0	1				

HIDEBOUND (IRE)

7 b g Buckskin (FR) - Merry Run (Deep Run)
OWNER: W.V. M.W. & Mrs E.S.ROBINS
TRAINER: N.J.HENDERSON. Lambourn, Berkshire
CAREER FORM FIGURES: 1 - 112
CAREER WINS: 1998: Apr CHELTENHAM Heavy NHF 2m 1f; Nov NEWBURY Gd/Sft NH 2m;
Dec ASCOT Soft NH 2m

Before his run in the Grade 1 Tolworth Hurdle at Sandown in January, Hidebound had looked as good a novice hurdler as there was on either side of the Irish Sea. Unfortunately, he proved no match for Henry Daly's Behrajan at the Esher track, finishing a well beaten sixteen lengths second. After appearing to be cantering at the second last, Hidebound suddenly hit a brick wall and only just held on for second place.

Subsequently, it transpired that the seven year old had a major nasal discharge and therefore a genuine reason for the performance. Earlier, he had destroyed what had looked a good field for a valuable Ascot novice which included the likes of Renzo, Salamah and Hoh Invader in December by upwards of seventeen lengths. This victory had come on the back of an equally impressive six lengths defeat of Billingsgate at Newbury.

Nicky Henderson has a magnificent team of horses for the 1999/2000 season, not least in the novice chase department with the likes of Easter Ross, King's Boy and Hidebound. However, it may be that the last named may prove to be the pick of the bunch. It is worth noting that Hidebound is, reportedly, not a difficult horse to get ready so he is worthy of support on his chasing debut regardless of the opposition.

POINTS TO NOTE
Probable Best Distance   -   2 miles
Preferred Going   -   Soft
Connection's Comments: "He is crying out to jump fences. He is a big horse but a very slick jumper, and he'll stay two and a half miles." N.HENDERSON

GOING:	R	W	P	TRACK:	R	W	P
Heavy	1	1	0	Left Handed	2	2	0
Soft	2	1	1	Right	2	1	1
Gd/Sft	1	1	0	Galloping	3	2	1
				Stiff/Undul.	1	1	0

TRIP:	R	W	P		R	W	P
2m	3	2	1	2m 1f	1	1	0

JETS TABS (IRE)

7 b g Roselier (FR) - Bell Walks Fancy (Entrechat)
OWNER: The JET STATIONERY COMPANY Ltd.
TRAINER: M.A.PITMAN. Upper Lambourn, Berkshire.
CAREER FORM FIGURES: 4211 - 1
CAREER WINS: 1997: Dec CHEPSTOW Heavy NHF 2m: 1998: Jan WINDSOR Gd/Sft MH 2¾m; Nov CHELTENHAM Gd/Sft HH 3¼m

From a personal point of view, I consider Jet Tabs to be one of the best handicapped hurdlers around at the moment. We may not have seen a great deal of him but what we have seen is enough to suggest he is a horse with a huge future.

A top class bumper horse two seasons ago when winning a Grade 2 event at Chepstow from the likes of Muskhill and King's Measure, he has won both his starts over hurdles to date. It was the second of those victories which really made one sit up and take notice, in a Cheltenham handicap over three and a quarter miles.

Making headway on the bridle with four flights to jump, Jet Tabs led approaching the last and effortlessly powered up the Cheltenham hill to register a very easy ten lengths win over Runaway Pete. He was subsequently raised eight pounds by the handicapper and, while many people will say he beat very little, it was the manner of his success which was so impressive. Injury meant the seven year old has not been seen since but off a rating of 120, I will be amazed if he cannot add to his victories this season over hurdles. Also, you cannot rule out the possibility of him developing into a Stayers' Hurdle contender such is the improvement he is open to.

Jet Tabs was bought for just Ir10,000gns as a four year old and he already looks a bargain and that is even before he starts his real job, chasing.

POINTS TO NOTE
Probable Best Distance   -   3 miles +
Preferred Going   -   Good / Soft
Connection's Comments: "He will remain over hurdles for the time being and I would be disappointed if he couldn't win off his current mark." M.PITMAN.

GOING:	R	W	P	TRACK:	R	W	P
Heavy	1	1	0	Figure of 8	1	1	0
Soft	1	0	1	Left Handed	3	2	1
Gd/Sft	2	2	0	Right	1	0	0
Good	1	0	0	Galloping	1	0	0
				Stiff/Undul.	3	2	1
				Tight	1	1	0

TRIP:	R	W	P		R	W	P
2m	3	1	1	3m 2f	1	1	0
2m 6f	1	1	0				

KING OF THE CASTLE (IRE)

4 b g Cataldi - Monashuna (Boreen (FR))
OWNER: Mr ROBERT HITCHINS
TRAINER: M.A.PITMAN. Upper Lambourn, Berkshire.
CAREER FORM FIGURES: 11
CAREER WINS: 1999: Mar FOLKESTONE Gd/Sft NHF 2m 1f; Apr AINTREE Good NHF 2m

Nahthen Lad may not have won the Grand National but the script could not have been better written as Jenny Pitman's final runner at Aintree proved to be a winning one as King of the Castle won the £13,200 Grade 2 Martell Champion bumper. And what a horse he looks on the strength of two very impressive victories.

The son of Cataldi had been well touted prior to his racecourse debut and was sent off a warm 7/4 favourite at Folkestone in March. During the race, he was always moving well and took up the running with a furlong to travel. He rapidly asserted his authority and was a hard held winner at the line by four lengths from the staying on El Monty. King of the Castle was again well supported next time (7/2 from 5/1), in the valuable Aintree bumper, and he again made sure the money did not remain in the bookmakers's satchels with a most authoritative performance. Confidently ridden by Mark Pitman's excellent young jockey Liam Corcoran, he sliced through the field on the bridle and took charge at the quarter mile pole. Despite edging left inside the final furlong, the four year old ran out an extremely impressive winner by four lengths from Errand Boy.

King of the Castle is another outstanding prospect Mark Pitman takes charge of from his now retired mother and being only four, he is a horse with a very bright future. Being a tall gelding, chasing will be his game but he will win more than his share of novice hurdles this season. The only slight query about him is regarding the type of track. He possesses an awful lot of speed and looked tailormade for Aintree. Whether he will be quite so effective at Cheltenham remains to be seen.

POINTS TO NOTE

Probable Best Distance - 2 miles
Preferred Going - Good
Connection's Comments: "He is a very nice horse with a good turn of foot." Mrs J.PITMAN OBE

GOING:	R	W	P	TRACK:	R	W	P
Gd/Sft	1	1	0	Left Handed	1	1	0
Good	1	1	0	Right	1	1	0
				Tight	1	1	0
				Tight/Undul.	1	1	0

TRIP:	R	W	P		R	W	P
2m	1	1	0	2m 1f	1	1	0

KING'S ROAD (IRE)

6 b g King's Ride - Live Aid (Little Buskins)
OWNER: Mrs NICHOLAS JONES
TRAINER: N.A.TWISTON-DAVIES. Naunton, Gloucestershire.
CAREER FORM FIGURES: 31611 - 121341
CAREER WINS: 1998: Feb HAYDOCK Soft NHF 2m; Apr AINTREE Soft NHF 2m;
PUNCHESTOWN Heavy NHF 2m; Nov CHEPSTOW Gd/Sft NH 2m 4f: 1999: Jan NEWBURY
Heavy NH 2m 5f; Apr AINTREE Good NH 3m

Bought for just 16,000gns at the 1997 Doncaster May Sales by Paul Webber on behalf of Nigel Twiston-Davies, King's Road has proved a real bargain. He has already won three bumpers and three novices hurdles and now he is due to embark on his chasing career and he is expected to make a top class novice this season.

Stamina is undoubtedly the key to King's Road. He loves soft ground and, as he showed by winning the valuable Belle Epoque Sefton Novices' Hurdle at Aintree last April, he stays three miles extremely well and will get further if necessary. Two and a half miles on good or even good to soft and he is definitely vulnerable to 'speed' horses. The other key to his successes is his toughness. He is a horse who never knows when he is beaten as he displayed at Aintree. Despite mistakes at two of the last three hurdles, he fought off each opponent who threatened his lead producing one of the gamest efforts you are ever likely to see.

Earlier in the year, King's Road had beaten Buck's Palace by ten lengths in a Chepstow novice and then Rio's King by two lengths in the Challow Hurdle at Newbury. Following that he chased home Behrajan at Warwick and then Barton in the Royal & Sun Alliance Hurdle at Cheltenham. On each occasion, neither had presented a stiff enough test of stamina for King's Road.

Despite the fact the six year old is inclined to clatter the odd hurdle, King's Road has the scope and the build for jumping fences and already the Royal & Sun Alliance Chase must be high on connection's list of priorities for this season.

POINTS TO NOTE
Probable Best Distance   -   3 miles +
Preferred Going   -   Soft / Heavy
Connection's Comments: "Although we haven't schooled him over fences yet, he could be a brilliant prospect for chasing." N.TWISTON-DAVIES

GOING:	R	W	P	TRACK:	R	W	P
Heavy	2	2	0	Left Handed	7	4	1
Soft	2	2	0	Right	4	2	2
Gd/Sft	3	1	1	Galloping	4	2	2
Good	4	1	2	Stiff/Undul.	3	1	0
				Tight	3	3	0
				Tight/Undul.	1	0	1

TRIP:	R	W	P		R	W	P
2m	5	3	1	2m 6f	1	0	1
2m 4f	2	1	1	3m	1	1	0
2m 5f	2	1	0				

KIT SMARTIE (IRE)

7 b g Be My Native (USA) - Smart Cookie (Lord Gayle (USA))
OWNER: Mr D.M.FORSTER
TRAINER: D.M.FORSTER. Heighington, Co.Durham.
CAREER FORM FIGURES: 63 - 38513111
CAREER WINS: 1998: Jan HUNTINGDON Gd/Sft HH 2m 5f; Mar SEDGEFIELD Gd/Sft NH 2m
5f; Apr AYR Good NH 2¾m; PERTH Gd/Sft NH 3m

Having selected Kit Smartie in the Top 50 Prospects of last year's edition of *One Jump Ahead*, it was particularly disappointing that he failed to run at all last term. The reason being that he had a leg infection. However, he retains his position in this season's edition because of the huge potential he has shown.

Following four victories, he achieved a handicap mark of 122 and the most interesting aspect from last season was that Donald Forster actually gave him an entry in the Stayers' Hurdle. The trainer clearly thinks there is still a lot better to come. Norman Williamson who is unbeaten on the horse in two runs, is reportedly very keen on him and sees his future over fences.

The latest news from the Forster stable is that Kit Smartie is now 100% once again and he will be going novice chasing this term. All being well, he will be back on a racecourse by the beginning of November when there is some give in the ground. If taking to fences then he wouldn't have to improve considerably to be near top class as, on his hurdling form, he comfortably beat the likes of Marlborough, Lord of the River and Supreme Charm.

Purchased as a yearling by Forster, Kit Smartie could really put the County Durham handler well and truly on the training map this term. His chasing debut is eagerly awaited.

POINTS TO NOTE

Probable Best Distance	-	**3 miles**
Preferred Going	-	**Good / Soft**

Connection's Comments: "He is fine now and will go straight novice chasing this season."
D.FORSTER

GOING:	R	W	P	TRACK:	R	W	P
Gd/Sft	4	3	0	Left Handed	5	2	1
Good	3	1	1	Right	5	2	2
Gd/Fm	3	0	2	Galloping	4	2	1
				Stiff/Undul.	2	0	1
				Tight	3	1	1
				Tight/Undul.	1	1	0

TRIP:	R	W	P		R	W	P
2m	3	0	1	2m 5f	2	2	0
2m 1f	1	0	1	2m 6f	1	1	0
2m 4f	1	0	0	3m	2	1	1

LORD OF THE SKY

6 b g Lord Bud - Fardella (ITY) (Molvedo)
OWNER: Mr S.E.CONSTABLE
TRAINER: L.LUNGO. Carrutherstown, Dumfriesshire.
CAREER FORM FIGURES: 1 - 11
CAREER WINS: 1998: Mar WETHERBY Gd/Sft PTP 3m; Nov AYR Gd/Sft NHF 2m; HEXHAM
Heavy NHF 2m

Lenny Lungo enjoyed a fantastic season last year sending out fifty six winners and one horse who
contributed two of those victories is the very exciting Lord of the Sky.

He was bought privately out of Yorkshire point to point trainer Tim Walford's yard, having won
his only start 'between the flags' by two lengths at his local track Wetherby. Walford had
reportedly gone on record saying he was "the best horse I have ever trained." Lord of the Sky
made an immediate impact for his new connections when winning a competitive looking Ayr
bumper by a length and a quarter from the well thought of Lingdale Lad.

However, it was his next start which will stick in the memory. It came, again in a bumper, at
Hexham. Clearly relishing the testing conditions, the son of Lord Bud absolutely annihilated the
opposition without Robbie Supple really having to ask his mount a serious question. In fact, he
was heavily eased inside the final furlong and yet still won by a long looking eight lengths. "He
won on good ground at Ayr, and on heavy ground with a penalty here, so that proves he's above
average," remarked his trainer afterwards.

Unfortunately, Lord of the Sky was found to be quite stiff afterwards and was wisely given the
rest of the season off. Lenny Lungo feels he will be even better once stepped up in trip and he
looks sure to be a force in all the North's top novice hurdles this term.

POINTS TO NOTE
Probable Best Distance   -   2½miles +
Preferred Going   -   Soft
Connection's Comments: "He is a real prospect for some of the big novice hurdles this
season." L.LUNGO

GOING:	R	W	P	TRACKS:	R	W	P
Heavy	1	1	0	Left Handed	3	3	0
Gd/Sft	2	2	0	Galloping	1	1	0
				Stiff/Undul.	1	1	0
				Tight	1	1	0

TRIP:	R	W	P		R	W	P
2m	2	2	0	3m	1	1	0

MAJOR SPONSOR (IRE)
7 b g Strong Gale - Hue 'n' Cry (IRE) (Denel (FR))
OWNER: S.P.GRAHAM Ltd
TRAINER: G.M.MOORE. Middleham, North Yorkshire.
CAREER FORM FIGURES: 9 - 9356113 - 121123
CAREER WINS: 1998: Mar DOWN ROYAL Good NHF 2m; DOWNPATRICK Yielding NHF 2¼m; Oct SOUTHWELL Good NH 2m: 1999: Jan CATTERICK Good NH 2m 3f; NEWCASTLE Soft NH 2m

George Moore enjoyed his best season for many years last term when training thirty four winners with his win and place prize-money amounting to £164,982. The 1999/2000 season promises to be just as good for the Middleham trainer with a number of promising novice chasers which are headed by the ex-Jeremy Maxwell trained Major Sponsor.

Major Sponsor won two Irish points plus two bumpers (also placed behind the ill-fated Cardinal Hill) whilst in the care of Maxwell. Owned by Northern Ireland bookmaker Sean Graham, he looks a most exciting prospect. He won three of his six starts last term with the highlight undoubtedly being his thirteen lengths demolition of Lord Lamb at Newcastle in January. Making all, he never looked like being headed and won as he pleased. His previous wins for Moore had been just as emphatic, as he beat Damza by twenty five lengths at Southwell and Corporation Pop by fifteen lengths at Catterick.

Major Sponsor did have the misfortune, in his three defeats, to come up against Crazy Horse (twice) and Barton and, while on each occasion he was comprehensively beaten, he was far from disgraced. Rated 137 over hurdles, the seven year old did particularly well for a horse who is essentially a chaser in the making.

Being a winning pointer over three miles you would expect Major Sponsor to stay very well but he certainly has plenty of speed and two miles, as he showed at Newcastle, holds no fears for him. He is likely to develop into one of the North's top novice chasers this season and must be followed.

POINTS TO NOTE
Probable Best Distance - 2 - 2½ miles
Preferred Going - Good / Soft
Connection's Comments: "He's going novice chasing and he's a very exciting prospect for that." S.GRAHAM

GOING:	R	W	P	TRACK:	R	W	P
Heavy	3	0	2	Left Handed	9	3	4
Soft	3	1	1	Right	5	2	1
Yldng	2	1	0	Galloping	10	2	4
Good	5	3	2	Tight	1	1	0
Gd/Fm	1	0	0	Tight/Undul.	3	2	1

TRIP:	R	W	P		R	W	P
2m	8	3	3	2m 3f	1	1	0
2m 2f	4	1	1	2m 4f	1	0	1

MARLBOROUGH (IRE)

7 br g Strong Gale - Wrekenogan (Tarqogan)
OWNER: Mr R.OGDEN CBE
TRAINER: H.D.J.DALY. Ludlow, Shropshire.
CAREER FORM FIGURES: 5213 - U111FF
CAREER WINS: 1998: Mar NEWBURY Gd/Sft MH 2m 5f; Nov WORCESTER Heavy NC 2m 4f;
Dec LINGFIELD Soft NC 3m: 1999: Jan KEMPTON Soft NC 3m

Despite failing to complete in half of his six races over fences last term, I have no hesitation in nominating Marlborough as a chaser to follow this season. By and large, Marlborough is a safe and accurate jumper and his falls can be attributed to the fact he was still a relatively weak and inexperienced horse who will have benefited greatly from another Summer at grass. Bearing in mind, he took on some of the best staying novice chasers last season, he is attractively handicapped on a mark of 125.

Marlborough's chasing debut at Towcester in October really showed what ability he retains. Leading at the sixth, Richard Johnson's mount slipped and was headed at the tenth and appeared to have lost all chance. However, once given time he was back amongst the leaders when finally unseating his rider at the third last. He must be some horse to make up so much ground in such a short space of time. Clearly unaffected by such an experience, Marlborough reeled off a hat-trick of wins at Worcester (by twelve lengths), Lingfield (by twenty two lengths) and Kempton (by nine lengths). The son of Strong Gale would have made it four but for falling at the second last at Haydock with the race at his mercy. Marlborough's final start came in the Grade 2 Reynoldstown Novices' Chase at Ascot and, again, he held every chance when parting company with Richard Dunwoody at the last when upsides Lord of the River. Despite Jamie Osborne's claims that he would have won anyway, it is very difficult to call the likely outcome.

After such mishaps, it is likely Henry Daly will be looking for a confidence boosting win at one of the minor tracks to begin with this season but there is no reason why Marlborough cannot develop into a serious contender for all the major staying handicap chasers. Make no mistake, he is a horse with tremendous ability and potential.

POINTS TO NOTE

Probable Best Distance — 3 miles
Preferred Going — Soft
Connection's Comments: "He is a horse who will improve as he gets older." M.FITZGERALD

GOING:	R	W	P	TRACK:	R	W	P
Heavy	2	1	1	Left Handed	7	3	2
Soft	4	2	0	Right	3	1	0
Gd/Sft	2	1	0	Galloping	6	2	2
Good	2	0	1	Stiff/Undul.	1	0	0
				Tight	1	1	0
				Tight/Undul.	2	1	0

TRIP:	R	W	P		R	W	P
2m 4f	3	1	0	2m 6f	2	0	1
2m 5f	2	1	1	3m	3	2	0

MINUIT NOIR (IRE)

3 b g Machiavellian (USA) - Misbegotten (IRE) (Baillamont (USA))
OWNER: MARQUESA de MORATALLA
TRAINER: J.G.FITZGERALD. Norton, North Yorkshire.
CAREER FORM FIGURES: (Flat 1999) 31
CAREER WIN: (Flat 1999) Jul PONTEFRACT Gd/Sft Mdn 1¼ m

It is very unusual for an ex-Flat horse to feature in the Top 50 of *One Jump Ahead* but Jimmy FitzGerald is very excited by the prospect of sending Minuit Noir juvenile hurdling this season.

Unraced as a two year old, Minuit Noir made his racecourse debut at York in June in a mile maiden. Having been outpaced early on, he stayed on strongly to claim third spot behind Bryan McMahon's The Exhibition Fox. The son of Machiavellian was then stepped up in trip for another maiden, this time at Pontefract a month later. Always close to the pace, Willie Supple's mount took up the running inside the final furlong and comfortably held the late challenge of Clive Brittain's Bellefonte by half a length.

A very laid back horse, Minuit Noir is ideally suited by some cut in the ground. Jimmy FitzGerald has trained some tremendous juvenile hurdlers in the past with names such as Sybillin readily springing to mind and it wouldn't be at all surprising if Minuit Noir turns out to be very good as well.

POINTS TO NOTE

Probable Best Distance	-	2 miles
Preferred Going	-	Good / Soft

Connection's Comments: "He is a lovely horse and will make a nice jumper this season."
J.FITZGERALD

(1999 Flat Season):

GOING:	R	W	P	TRACK:	R	W	P
Gd/Sft	2	1	1	Left Handed	2	1	1
				Galloping	1	0	1
				Stiff/Undul.	1	1	0

MONARCH'S PURSUIT

5 b g Pursuit of Love - Last Detail (Dara Monarch)
OWNER: Mrs JEAN P.CONNEW
TRAINER: T.D.EASTERBY. Great Habton, North Yorkshire.
CAREER FORM FIGURES: 115 - 8
CAREER WINS: 1997: Oct WETHERBY Gd/Fm NH 2m; Nov WETHERBY Gd/Fm NH 2m

Despite showing very little on the Flat, Monarch's Pursuit looked a very good hurdler in the making two seasons ago by winning his first two starts over jumps at Wetherby, including a Grade 2 event. Unfortunately, we have not seen a great deal of him since but that is largely due to the fact he has been given time to develop.

A big rangy son of Pursuit of Love with plenty of scope, he only ran once last season finishing a disappointing last of eight to Tyrolean Dream, again at the West Yorkshire track in October. However, he was still a weak and immature horse, and he was given the rest of the season off. On the best of his form from two years ago, Monarch's Pursuit should make a very exciting novice chaser over the minimum trip.

He beat Dulas Bay by seven lengths on his hurdling debut and then followed that up by scoring by a head from Martin Pipe's Amitge. Rounding off his juvenile campaign, the five year old was fifth to Real Estate at Ascot. His three starts saw him earn a rating of 120.

As everyone knows, both Peter and now Tim Easterby have done particularly well with their novice chasers and it is not difficult to see him running up a sequence of wins before going on to even better things.

POINTS TO NOTE
Probable Best Distance   -   2 miles
Preferred Going   -   Good
Connection's Comments: "He is a natural jumper and one day will make a very, very good chaser." T.EASTERBY

GOING:	R	W	P	TRACK:	R	W	P
Gd/Sft	1	0	0	Left Handed	3	2	0
Good	1	0	0	Right	1	0	0
Gd/Fm	2	2	0	Galloping	1	0	0
				Tight	3	2	0

TRIP:	R	W	P
2m	4	2	0

MR LAMB
4 gr g Deploy - Caroline Lamb (Hotfoot)
OWNER: Mr D.A.JOHNSON
TRAINER: M.C.PIPE. Nicholashayne, Somerset.
CAREER FORM FIGURES: 1
CAREER WIN: 1999: Jan MUSSELBURGH Gd/Sft NHF 2m

Martin Pipe had to go to 125,000gns at the Doncaster January Sales to secure the purchase of the ex-Sally Hall trained Mr Lamb. A half-brother to Mary Reveley's Lord Lamb, he won his sole start last term whilst under the guidance of the Middleham trainer.

Mr Lamb had always been well thought of by the Hall team and was backed, accordingly, on his racecourse debut (7/2 from 4/1) at Musselburgh in January. Prominent throughout, he led at the two furlong pole and ran on strongly to beat the subsequent dual winner Barney Knows by two and a half lengths. Interestingly, Colin Platt, who was representing Miss Hall, stated afterwards: "He is better than Lord Lamb was at the same stage, he has more toe. He is still a big baby who will improve for the run." It was therefore little wonder that Mr Lamb was bought for such a hefty price at the following sale.

Mr Lamb did not actually see a racecourse for his new connections but, significantly, he was due to run in the Aintree Champion bumper on Grand National day but was withdrawn at the overnight stage. However, taking into account Colin Platt's comments above, Mr Lamb will have benefited enormously from another Summer behind him and will make a high class novice hurdler this season.

POINTS TO NOTE

Probable Best Distance	-	**2 miles**
Preferred Going	-	**Good**

Connection's Comments: "He's a nice horse, and looked quite useful when he won at Musselburgh, showing a decent turn of foot." M.PIPE

GOING:	R	W	P	TRACK:	R	W	P
Gd/Sft	1	1	0	Right	1	1	0
				Tight	1	1	0

TRIP:	R	W	P
2m	1	1	0

MULKEV PRINCE (IRE)

8 b g Lancastrian - Waltzing Shoon (Green Shoon)
OWNER: Mr W.M.G.BLACK
TRAINER: J.H.JOHNSON. Crook, Co. Durham.
CAREER FORM FIGURES: 63 - 0R1R23 - 3RFP24P - 6122172 - F545P2
CAREER WINS: 1996: Feb FAIRYHOUSE Gd/Yld MH 2¼ m: 1997: Nov THURLES Yld/Sft NC 2m : 1998: Feb FAIRYHOUSE Yld/Sft NC 2m

The fact Mulkev Prince is a sketchy jumper and has run out on three occasions is hardly the ingredient of a horse to follow. However, Howard Johnson's handicap chaser is a horse with an awful lot more ability than he has shown yet for his new connections.

Bought out of Ger Lyons' yard at the 1998 Doncaster August Sales for 42,000gns, Mulkev Prince proved last season a classic case of an ex-Irish horse who has taken a year to fully acclimatise. As a result of five out of six disappointing runs for Johnson, he has steadily slipped down the handicap. Having begun the season on a mark of 130, he is now rated 116 and when you consider the form he showed in Ireland as a novice two years ago, then he is extremely well handicapped.

Two seasons ago, Mulkev Prince won a Grade 2 Novices' Chase at Fairyhouse by two lengths from the very useful Delphi Lodge and he also finished four lengths second to his now stablemate Direct Route in a Grade 1 event at the Punchestown Festival. Having arrived in Britain with a big reputation, he disappointed badly for Howard Johnson and was clearly taking some time to adjust to the British fences, falling at Ascot and making numerous mistakes on his other outings. He ran his best race at Huntingdon on his final outing of the season when chasing home Ferdy Murphy's Oscail An Doras in March.

The latest news from the Howard Johnson camp is that Mulkev Prince has Summered "tremendously well" and he is expected to make up some of that expensive price tag in no uncertain terms this season.

POINTS TO NOTE
Probable Best Distance   -   2 miles
Preferred Going   -   Soft
Connection's Comments: "He has slipped down the handicap and we will now be able to run him in the North a bit more often, although he must go right handed." H.JOHNSON

GOING:	R	W	P	TRACK:	R	W	P
Heavy	4	0	2	Left Handed	4	0	1
Soft	2	0	1	Right	24	3	8
Yld/Sft	5	2	1	Galloping	20	2	7
Ylding	2	0	0	Tight	2	0	0
Gd/Yld	4	1	0	Tight/Undul.	6	1	2
Gd/Sft	2	0	0				
Good	6	0	3				
Gd/Fm	2	0	1				
Firm	1	0	1				

TRIP:	R	W	P		R	W	P
2m	15	2	5	2m 4f	9	0	3
2m 2f	4	1	1				

NERVOUS O'TOOLE (IRE)
4 b g Mister Lord (USA) - Dooney's Daughter (The Parson)
OWNER: Mrs M.BONE
TRAINER: M.A.PITMAN. Upper Lambourn, Berkshire.
CAREER FORM FIGURES: 1
CAREER WIN: 1999: May WORCESTER Gd/Sft NHF 2m

Many readers will recall that Jenny Pitman introduced her top class staying hurdler Princeful at Worcester in May 1996. During the same month earlier this year, at the same venue, she introduced another potential star in the shape of Nervous O'Toole.

By the increasingly popular sire Mister Lord, Nervous O'Toole produced a mightily impressive performance to beat eighteen rivals by upwards of six lengths but it could have been considerably more had Liam Corcoran not sat motionless for the majority of the home straight.

Such was the manner of the success, it has left his connections contemplating a tilt at the Festival bumper at Cheltenham and therefore shelving his novice hurdling career for another season. The prospect of that happening must be further enhanced by the fact Nervous O'Toole is a full brother to Mark Pitman's Festival bumper winner of last season Monsignor. It would be quite a double if two brothers could win the race in successive years.

Wide margin bumper winners are very difficult to assess but one has the feeling we witnessed the start of a very successful career for Nervous O'Toole at Worcester last May.

POINTS TO NOTE

Probable Best Distance	-	2 - 2½ miles
Preferred Going	-	Good / Soft

Connection's Comments: "He is a very nice horse and we may well aim him at the Cheltenham bumper." M.PITMAN

GOING:	R	W	P	TRACK:	R	W	P
Gd/Sft	1	1	0	Left Handed	1	1	0
				Galloping	1	1	0

TRIP:	R	W	P
2m	1	1	0

NORLANDIC (NZ)

7 ch g First Norman (USA) - April Snow (NZ) (Icelandic)
OWNER: The TILL HOUSE PARTNERSHIP
TRAINER: P.J.HOBBS. Minehead, Somerset.
CAREER FORM FIGURES: 06 - 3 - 5521511
CAREER WINS: 1999: Feb TAUNTON Gd/Sft HH 3m; Mar EXETER Good HC 2m 7f; Apr EXETER Gd/Sft NHC 2m 7f

Having selected Philip Hobbs' In The Blood to develop into a useful handicap chaser last season, it was particularly satisfying to see him win four on the trot. This year, the Somerset trainer looks to have a very similar type in the lightly raced Norlandic. Unbeaten in two starts over fences, he looks one step ahead of the handicapper on a mark of 109.

Norlandic displayed progressive form over hurdles, winning a Taunton handicap in February by one and three quarter lengths from Mister Generosity. However, it was as a chaser that we were always likely to see the best of the seven year old. He produced a fine performance on his chasing debut to beat the consistent Country Store by a length and a quarter at Exeter. And, despite a thirteen pounds hike in the weights, Norlandic won his second start over fences, again at Exeter, by a facile nine lengths from Joy For Life. Robert Widger's mount was always travelling well and his rider was able to ease him almost to a walk on the run-in. He has subsequently been raised by the handicapper a further thirteen pounds but the son of First Norman is still very much one to follow.

Norlandic is open to any amount of improvement this season, although Philip Hobbs did stress earlier in the season that he is a horse who needs some cut in the ground. He is a staying handicap chaser to watch closely.

POINTS TO NOTE

Probable Best Distance	-	3 miles
Preferred Going	-	Good / Soft

Connection's Comments: "He is a very progressive chaser." P.HOBBS

GOING:	R	W	P		TRACK:	R	W	P
Soft	3	0	1		Left Handed	3	0	0
Gd/Sft	4	2	0		Right	7	3	2
Good	3	1	1		Galloping	1	0	0
					Stiff/Undul.	4	2	1
					Tight	3	1	1
					Tight/Undul.	2	0	0

TRIP:	R	W	P			R	W	P
2m	1	0	0					
2m 3f	1	0	0		2m 6f	2	0	1
2m 4f	1	0	0		2m 7f	2	2	0
2m 5f	1	0	1		3m	2	1	0

OCTOBER MIST (IRE)
5 gr g Roselier (FR) - Bonny Joe (Derring Rose)
OWNER: Mrs M.B.SCHOLEY
TRAINER: Mrs G.R.REVELEY. Lingdale, Cleveland.
CAREER FORM FIGURES: 2

Mary Reveley is known to be particularly keen on the prospects of October Mist this season. Considered to be weak and immature last year, he still displayed an abundance of promise in his sole outing, a Wetherby bumper.

It came at the popular West Yorkshire track's Sunday fixture in October and, despite it being his racecourse debut, the son of Roselier was well supported in the market being backed from 6/1 into 9/2. Having travelled supremely well, Peter Niven's mount looked set for victory passing the two furlong pole. However, a combination of greenness, which led to October Mist hanging to his right, and a tough and resolute rival in the more experienced Knockara Fair, led to him finishing second, two lengths behind Alistair Charlton's charge. Despite his defeat, Mary Reveley must have been delighted with his effort, especially as the pair had drawn ten lengths clear of the subsequent dual winner Ackzo.

October Mist has an equally good pedigree to back up his ability being a half brother to Robert Alner's above average hurdler Who Am I and from the family of the high class two mile chaser Lord Dorcet.

He has been given plenty of time to develop since his Wetherby run and the plan is for him to have another run in a bumper before going novice hurdling. A very interesting prospect.

POINTS TO NOTE
Probable Best Distance	-	2 - 2½ miles
Preferred Going	-	Good / Soft

Connection's Comments: "This is a lovely horse and we like him very much. We've been very patient as the Roselier's never come to themselves until they're older." Mrs M.REVELEY

GOING:	R	W	P		TRACK:	R	W	P
Soft	1	0	1		Left Handed	1	0	1
					Tight	1	0	1
TRIP:	R	W	P					
2m	1	0	1					

OVER THE WATER (IRE)

7 gr g Over The River (FR) - Shanacloon Lass (General Ironside)
OWNER: The DROOP PARTNERS
TRAINER: R.H.ALNER. Blandford, Dorset.
CAREER FORM FIGURES: P267 - 9363 - 11
CAREER WINS: 1998: Nov KEMPTON Soft NC 2m 4f; WINCANTON Good NC 2m 5f

What a difference a fence can make ! It certainly has as far as Over The Water is concerned. As his form figures suggest, he was only a moderate hurdler but once he was sent chasing last season, the seven year old proved a revelation. In many ways, it should come as no surprise as Over The Water was bought by Robert Alner from Tom Costello in Ireland, who has supplied the Dorset trainer with so many good chasers.

The son of Over The River jumped beautifully on his chasing debut when slamming the highly regarded Supreme Charm by twenty five lengths at Kempton. Despite Kim Bailey's claims that his charge hated the soft ground, there was no disputing the ease with which Over The Water won. He was not quite as impressive next time but still beat Kentish Bard by two lengths at Wincanton on ground which was probably plenty fast enough for him. Unfortunately, Over The Water picked up an injury soon afterwards and has not reappeared since.

However, while his connections probably wouldn't have agreed at the time, the injury may prove to be a blessing in disguise as he is now an extremely well handicapped staying chaser for this season. Rated just 100, he looks just the type to run up a sequence, especially if stepped up to three miles for the first time.

POINTS TO NOTE

Probable Best Distance	-	3 miles
Preferred Going	-	Soft

Connection's Comments: "To win so well on a Grade 1 track (Kempton) suggests he's a horse with a real future, and I don't think he's just a mud-lover. He has a lovely action, a great attitude, and I'm sure he has a lot of improvement in him." R.ALNER

GOING:	R	W	P		TRACK:	R	W	P
Soft	1	1	0		Figure of 8	1	0	0
Gd/Sft	2	0	0		Right	9	2	3
Good	6	1	3		Galloping	4	1	1
Gd/Fm	1	0	0		Tight	4	1	2
					Tight/Undul.	2	0	0
TRIP:	R	W	P			R	W	P
2m	1	0	0		2m 4f	2	1	0

| 2m 1f | 1 | 0 | 0 | 2m 5f | 1 | 1 | 0 |
| 2m 3f | 2 | 0 | 2 | 2m 6f | 3 | 0 | 1 |

PROMINENT PROFILE (IRE)
6 ch g Mazaad - Nakuru (IRE) (Mandalus)
OWNER: The SON PARTNERSHIP
TRAINER: N.A.TWISTON-DAVIES. Naunton, Gloucestershire.
CAREER FORM FIGURES: 10113034
CAREER WINS: 1998: Oct CHELTENHAM Gd/Sft NHF 2m; Dec CHEPSTOW Heavy NHF 2m:
1999: Jan WETHERBY Soft NH 2 1/2m

So often it is the case that untidy jumpers of hurdles tend to make superb jumpers of fences. More often that not it applies to big horses who find hurdles too small and would sooner kick them out of the way rather than jump them fluently. The late Mr Mulligan was a classic example. Prominent Profile is selected with the above theory very much in mind.

Prominent Profile began his career by running in Irish point to points. Having finished second at Taylorstown he then recorded a very impressive success at Lennymore in May 1998. *The Irish Field* reporter Margie McCloone stated: "He put in an exhibition round of jumping to win by twenty lengths." He was subsequently bought by the Twiston-Davies team.

While not quite reaching the top level, the son of Mazaad looked a very good hurdler last season for his new connections. He won two bumpers, including a Grade 2 event at Chepstow beating the likes of Frosty Canyon and Queen's Harbour by upwards of six lengths, and a novice hurdle at Wetherby. Prominent Profile was particularly impressive there, scoring from Master Pilgrim by a long looking ten lengths.

The six year old then took on some of the smartest novices around, finishing third to Premier Generation at Kempton, Barton at Aintree and fourth to Native Upmanship at the Punchestown Festival. Prominent Profile has yet to race beyond two and a half miles under Rules but his style of racing would suggest he would be even more effective over three miles. The Royal & Sun Alliance Chase rather than the Arkle Trophy is likely to be his ultimate target at the Cheltenham Festival this season. He does appear to go well fresh.

POINTS TO NOTE

Probable Best Distance	-	2½ miles +
Preferred Going	-	Soft

GOING:	R	W	P	TRACK:	R	W	P
Heavy	1	1	0	Left Handed	6	3	1
Soft	2	1	1	Right	2	0	1
Gd/Sft	3	1	0	Galloping	1	0	0
Yldng	1	0	0	Stiff/Undul.	4	2	0
Good	1	0	1	Tight	3	1	2

TRIP:	R	W	P		R	W	P
2m	5	2	1	2m 4f	3	1	1

QUEEN'S HARBOUR (IRE)

5 b g Brush Aside (USA) - Queenie Kelly (The Parson)
OWNER: Mr PHILIP MATTON
TRAINER: M.A.PITMAN. Upper Lambourn, Berkshire.
CAREER FORM FIGURES: 1314
CAREER WINS: 1998: Dec TOWCESTER Soft NHF 2m: 1999: Mar NEWBURY Soft NHF 2m

Queen's Harbour looked a horse of huge potential when winning on his racecourse debut at Towcester in December. He had clearly shown plenty of promise at home beforehand as he was well supported in the market from an opening 5/1 into 7/2. Leading two furlongs from home, he quickly put the issue beyond doubt as he sauntered home by thirteen lengths from Smoking Gun.

Following a good third to Prominent Profile at Chepstow later the same month, Queen's Harbour scored his second success. It came in a hotly contested affair at Newbury. Staying on gamely, under the guidance of Richard Dunwoody, he beat the newcomer Gunnerbe Posh by two and a half lengths with the very well thought of Lightning Strikes back in third. It was on the strength of that run that Jenny Pitman allowed the son of Brush Aside to take his place in the Festival bumper at Cheltenham and he ran some race.

Defying his huge odds of 40/1, Queen's Harbour arguably finished best of all to claim fourth position, six and a quarter lengths behind Mark Pitman's winner Monsignor. It was a most eyecatching run and he looks an excellent prospect for hurdling this term.

Being a half-brother to the smart but ill-fated stayer Ottowa, Queen's Harbour will be even more effective when stepped up to two and a half miles plus. Long term, he will make a smashing chaser but he is likely to make a high class novice hurdler in the meantime.

POINTS TO NOTE

Probable Best Distance   -   2½ miles +
Preferred Going   -   Soft
Connection's Comments: "Make no mistake, this is a very good horse." Mrs J.PITMAN OBE

GOING:	R	W	P	TRACK:	R	W	P
Heavy	1	0	1	Left Handed	3	1	1
Soft	2	2	0	Right	1	1	0
Gd/Sft	1	0	0	Galloping	1	1	0
				Stiff/Undul.	3	1	1

TRIP:	R	W	P
2m	4	2	1

RIO'S KING (IRE)

7 b g King's Ride - Rio Dulce (Rio Carmelo (FR))
OWNER: The GASCOIGNE BROOKES Partnership
TRAINER: J.C.TUCK. Didmarton, South Gloucestershire.
CAREER FORM FIGURES: 21 - 11325

CAREER WINS: 1998: Mar CHEPSTOW Gd/Sft NHF 2m; Nov WARWICK Soft NH 2m 3f; CHEPSTOW Gd/Sft NH 2½ m.

Robert Bellamy may be nearing the end of his riding career but he is unlikely to hang up his boots while Rio's King is still around. A big strong gelding who was placed in an Irish point to point, he has made excellent progress since joining John Tuck. He does, however, need to settle if he is to fulfil his undoubted potential.

An easy four lengths winner on his hurdling debut at Warwick from Siren Song in November was followed by an equally comfortable success over smart novices Irish Banker and Young Devereaux. Having pulled Bellamy's arms out for the first mile, Rio's King displayed a good turn of foot to wear down his rivals before going on to score by a length and a half. A good second to All Gong at Cheltenham in December was followed by an excellent effort behind King's Road in the Grade 1 Challow Hurdle at Newbury. The six year old looked set for victory jumping the final flight but he hung left and was outstayed by Nigel Twiston-Davies' durable gelding. You can forget Rio's King's final start as he was never travelling and came home a distant fifth of five behind Behrajan in a valuable novice at Warwick in February.

John Tuck has already schooled Rio's King over fences and he is understandably excited by the prospect of him going novice chasing this season. If he can learn to settle, there is no telling how far he could go up the chasing tree.

POINTS TO NOTE
Probable Best Distance	-	2½ miles +
Preferred Going	-	Soft

Connection's Comments: "We have schooled him at home and he jumps well. I like him a lot." J.TUCK

GOING:	R	W	P	TRACK:	R	W	P
Heavy	1	0	1	Left Handed	6	3	2
Soft	1	1	0	Right	1	0	1
Gd/Sft	3	2	0	Galloping	1	0	1
Good	1	0	1	Stiff/Undul.	3	2	1
Gd/Fm	1	0	1	Tight	1	0	1
				Tight/Undul.	2	1	0

TRIP:	R	W	P		R	W	P
2m	2	1	1	2m 4f	2	1	0
2m 1f	1	0	1	2m 5f	1	0	1
2m 3f	1	1	0				

SCOTIA NOSTRA (IRE)
7 b g High Estate - Crown Witness (Crowned Prince (USA))
OWNER: KINVALE PARTNERS
TRAINER: Miss V.M.WILLIAMS. Kings Caple, Hereford.
CAREER FORM FIGURES: 1400 - P112F52

CAREER WINS: 1997: Dec THURLES Sft/Hvy MH 2m: 1998: Nov AYR Gd/Sft NHC 2m 5f; CARLISLE Heavy NC 2½m.

In no way is the selection of Scotia Nostra a negative reflection of Jonjo O'Neill's training ability but Venetia Williams has, quite rightly, earned herself a reputation for improving other people's horses. On the best of his form last season, Scotia Nostra looks a potentially very well handicapped chaser on a rating of 111. Clearly, Miss Williams agrees as she paid 17,500gns for the son of High Estate at the Doncaster Spring Sales.

Previously trained in Ireland by Arthur Moore, he made a successful chasing debut last season for Jonjo O'Neill at Ayr. Jumping well, he led at the last and was pushed out to beat Phar Echo by three and a half lengths. He then followed that up with an equally convincing one and a quarter lengths victory over Menshaar at Carlisle. Despite a couple of indifferent efforts, Scotia Nostra did produce two more noteworthy performances last season. Firstly, he was beaten just half a length by King of Sparta at Cheltenham in December and, secondly, he ran a very sound race to finish second to Bouchasson in the Grade 2 Edinburgh Woollen Mill Future Champions' Chase at Ayr in April. Admittedly, he was beaten eighteen lengths by Philip Hobbs' charge but he was one and a half lengths ahead of the useful Irbee who is rated 131.

There were some doubts last season as to how resolute Scotia Nostra was but if Venetia Williams can bring about her usual improvement then we could find that the seven year old is at least a stone ahead of the handicapper. He is most definitely worth looking out for on his seasonal reappearance.

POINTS TO NOTE

| Probable Best Distance | - | 2 - 2½ miles |
| Preferred Going | - | Soft |

GOING:	R	W	P	TRACK:	R	W	P
Heavy	4	1	0	Left Handed	8	1	2
Sft/Hvy	1	1	0	Right	3	2	0
Soft	1	0	1	Galloping	6	1	1
Yld/Sft	1	0	0	Stiff/Undul.	3	1	1
Gd/Sft	3	1	0	Tight/Undul.	2	1	0
Good	1	0	1				

TRIP:	R	W	P		R	W	P
2m	4	1	0	2m 5f	4	1	1
2m 4f	3	1	1				

SPLENDID MELODY (IRE)
5 ch g Ile de Chypre - Slave-Lady (Menelek)
OWNER: Mr B.T.STEWART-BROWN
TRAINER: T.P.TATE. Tadcaster, North Yorkshire.
CAREER FORM FIGURES: 75311
CAREER WINS: 1999: Jan KELSO Heavy NH 2¼m; Feb CATTERICK Good NH 2m 3f.

In recent years, Tadcaster trainer Tom Tate has done particularly well with former Irish point to pointers, namely Ask Tom and Aghawadda Gold. His latest budding star from the same source is the five year old Splendid Melody.

In many ways, Splendid Melody has a very similar background to Ask Tom. Both horses were trained in Ireland by Tom Costello, both won an Irish point as a four year (Splendid Melody won at Liscarroll by a length (Gd/Sft) in March 1998 on his second start) and both were bought by Brian Stewart-Brown. However, whereas Ask Tom only won one hurdle race, the son of Ile de Chypre won twice over the smaller obstacles.

Splendid Melody did, admittedly, take time to adjust to British racing, finishing a well beaten seventh to Hidebound at Newbury and then only fifth to Kingennie at Newcastle. However, the five year old did then show some of his undoubted ability by chasing home the well regarded Tonoco at Haydock in December, just five and a quarter lengths behind in third. As a result, he was made an even money favourite for his next start at Kelso (both Ask Tom and Aghawadda Gold won there over hurdles) and he duly sluiced home by twenty three lengths. His jumping was immaculate. He then prevailed by a fast diminishing neck at Catterick on his final start from the subsequent dual winner Ackzo. Once again, his hurdling was first class but his performance did indicate one significant factor. Having gone three lengths clear at the second last and looking set for an comfortable victory, Splendid Melody did appear to tire appreciably on the run-in and even the sharp two miles three around Catterick seemed to stretch his stamina to the full. A drop back to two miles will be much more to his liking.

Splendid Melody's chasing debut this season is eagerly awaited. He has an excellent jumping technique, as you would expect coming from Tom Costello, he has pace and he is built like a chaser. Potentially top class.

POINTS TO NOTE

Probable Best Distance - **2 miles**
Preferred Going - **Good / Soft**
Connection's Comments: "He has plenty of pace and is a lovely prospect for chasing."
T.TATE

GOING:	R	W	P	TRACK:	R	W	P
Heavy	1	1	0	Left Handed	5	2	1
Soft	2	0	1	Galloping	2	0	0
Gd/Sft	1	0	0	Tight	1	0	1
Good	1	1	0	Tight/Undul.	2	2	0

TRIP:	R	W	P		R	W	P
2m	2	0	1	2m 3f	1	1	0
2m 2f	1	1	0	2m 4f	1	0	0

STAR OF DUNGANNON

6 b g Forzando - Key To The River (Irish River (FR))
OWNER: Mrs L.M.SEWELL
TRAINER: M.C.PIPE. Nicholashayne, Somerset.
CAREER FORM FIGURES: 2 - 2811
CAREER WINS: 1999: Feb KEMPTON Good NH 2m; Apr CHELTENHAM Good NH 2m 1f

Star of Dungannon retains his place in *One Jump Ahead,* following two very impressive wins in competitive looking novice hurdles. It is hoped and, expected, that he will develop into a major contender for all the big sponsored handicap hurdles such as the William Hill Hurdle at Sandown and the Tote Gold Trophy.

However, the key to Star of Dungannon is the going. He must have good to soft or quicker ground. Last season he encountered heavy ground at Chepstow for the first time and finished last of eight, beaten over eighty four lengths, by Prominent Profile in a Grade 2 bumper. When he made his hurdling debut at Kempton in February on good ground, the six year old looked a totally different horse. Travelling well throughout, he led at the second last, on the bridle, and quickly put the issue beyond doubt, striding four lengths clear of Leaburn. The surface was again riding good when Star of Dungannon won his second start over hurdles, this time at Cheltenham. For such an inexperienced horse to beat the three times winner Samakaan by five lengths was the performance of a highly promising and rapidly improving young hurdler.

Following his win at Prestbury Park, there was a lot of speculation that Star of Dungannon may be sent to Ireland for one of the big novice hurdles at the Punchestown Festival. However, that never transpired and it is probably highly significant that it didn't as had Star of Dungannon run the likes of Cardinal Hill close then his handicap mark for this season could have been ruined. Instead he should not be too harshly treated and is very much one to follow during 1999/2000.

POINTS TO NOTE

Probable Best Distance   -   2 miles
Preferred Going   -   Good
Connection's Comments: "He is a very nice horse who is sure to win lots more races."
M.PIPE

GOING:	R	W	P	TRACK:	R	W	P
Heavy	1	0	0	Left Handed	3	1	1
Gd/Sft	1	0	1	Right	2	1	1
Good	3	2	1	Galloping	1	0	1
				Stiff/Undul.	3	1	1
				Tight	1	1	0

TRIP:	R	W	P		R	W	P
2m	4	1	2	2m 1f	1	1	0

TOGGI DANCER (NZ)

6 b g Victory Dance - Solfatara (NZ) (Val du Fier (FR))
OWNER: ASHLEYBANK INVESTMENTS Ltd.
TRAINER: N.G.RICHARDS. Greystoke, Cumbria.
CAREER FORM FIGURES: 110
CAREER WINS: 1999: Jan AYR Heavy NHF 2m; Feb WARWICK Gd/Sft NHF 2m

Following the sad death of Gordon Richards last September, it was never going to be easy last season for his son Nicky. However, he begins this year with a 50 strong team made up largely of young unraced horses. One of his string who has already seen the racecourse on three occasions and looks a most promising individual is Toggi Dancer.

Bought by GWR for 20,000gns at the 1997 Doncaster Spring Sales, Toggi Dancer made an impressive winning debut in a bumper at Ayr. Ridden by the excellent amateur Mr J.Crowley, the six year old ploughed through the heavy ground to score by eight lengths from Cooladerry. Nicky Richards stated afterwards: "Everyone who has ridden him at home loves him and he's schooled so well that he wouldn't have been out of place in the novice chase today." Toggi Dancer then followed that victory up with an equally eyecatching success at Warwick in February. Taking up the running with just over a furlong to travel, he galloped on relentlessly to beat Henry Daly's Baie des Singes by half a dozen lengths. It was on the strength of these two wins that Nicky Richards allowed Toggi Dancer to take his chance in the Festival bumper at Cheltenham. While he never landed a blow at the principals on ground which was riding a touch too quick for him, he was far from disgraced in finishing about seventeen and a half lengths behind Monsignor in thirteenth place.

Like virtually all of Gordon Richards' purchases, Toggi Dancer is a future chaser but he will win his novice hurdles, particularly when stepped up in trip and when there is plenty of ease in the ground.

POINTS TO NOTE
Probable Best Distance   -   2½ miles +
Preferred Going   -   Soft
Connection's Comments: "I'm very excited about him." A.DOBBIN

GOING:	R	W	P	TRACK:	R	W	P
Heavy	1	1	0	Left Handed	3	2	0
Gd/Sft	2	1	0	Galloping	1	1	0
				Stiff/Undul.	1	0	0
				Tight/Undul.	1	1	0

TRIP:	R	W	P
2m	3	2	0

TONOCO

6 b g Teenoso (USA) - Lady Shoco (Montekin)
OWNER: Mr TREVOR HEMMINGS
TRAINER: Mrs S.J.SMITH. High Eldwick, West Yorkshire.
CAREER FORM FIGURES: 1 - 41116P
CAREER WINS: 1998: Apr AYR Good NHF 2m; Dec HAYDOCK Soft NH 2m: 1999: Jan
HUNTINGDON Soft NH 2m; Feb WETHERBY Good NH 2m

Ever since winning his bumper at Ayr in April 1998, the connections of Tonoco have longed for
the day the six year old went over fences. Despite two indifferent runs towards the end, Tonoco
enjoyed an excellent season over hurdles last term winning on three occasions and, in doing so,
achieved a handicap rating of 138.

Jumping well on his hurdling debut at Haydock in December he beat Beau by a comfortable four
lengths and then followed that up with a workmanlike one and a quarter lengths win over
Bacchanal at Huntingdon. Tonoco then completed his hat-trick with a narrow success over the
hugely talented, if somewhat quirky, Crazy Horse in a Grade 2 event at Wetherby. He displayed
tremendous determination, having been headed, to prevail by a neck from Lenny Lungo's
charge.

The son of Teenoso, reportedly, injured his off-fore when only sixth in the EBF Final at Sandown
in March and was certainly not himself when pulled up behind Barton at Aintree. He was never
really travelling that day and the run should be ignored.

Tonoco was a super jumper of hurdles and he should have no trouble taking to fences. Although
he has been tried over further, two miles looks his optimum at present and he is likely to take a
lot of beating in novice chases over the minimum trip, particularly in the North.

POINTS TO NOTE
Probable Best Distance   -   2 miles
Preferred Going   -   Good / Soft
Connection's Comments: "He is a very exciting horse and everything has been geared
towards his chasing career." Mrs S.SMITH

GOING:	R	W	P	TRACK:	R	W	P
Soft	4	2	0	Left Handed	5	3	0
Good	3	2	0	Right	2	1	0
				Galloping	4	2	0
				Tight	3	2	0

TRIP:	R	W	P		R	W	P
2m	5	4	0	2m 4f	2	0	0

TOTO TOSCATO (FR)

5 b g Lesotho (USA) - Tosca de Bellouet (FR) (Olmeto)
OWNER: Mrs H.J.CLARKE
TRAINER: D.NICHOLSON. Temple Guiting, Gloucestershire.
CAREER FORM FIGURES: (Excludes French form) 4113335
CAREER WINS: 1998: Nov CHEPSTOW Soft Hdle 2m; Dec ASCOT Soft Hdle 2m

Toto Toscato arrived at David Nicholson's Jackdaws Castle with a huge reputation having won two hurdles races at Auteuil in France worth an aggregate of £46,016. In his seven races for the 'Duke' last season, he won twice over hurdles but we will see the real Toto Toscato this year when he tackles fences for the first time. A big strong gelding, he has chaser written all over him.

The five year old's first victory on British soil was a mightily impressive five lengths beating of subsequent Arkle Chase winner Flagship Uberalles at Chepstow in November. He followed that up with a more workmanlike performance in beating City Hall by three quarters of a length at Ascot.

While it would be harsh to say Toto Toscato was disappointing in his next four starts, he did not progress in the manner expected. Undoubtedly his best effort from those four runs came when he ran a cracking race to finish sixteen lengths third to Sir Talbot and Decoupage in the Vincent O'Brien County Hurdle at the Cheltenham Festival.

Toto Toscato is very much 'a bridle horse.' He possesses a tremendously high cruising speed and such a quality can prove particularly potent over fences, as in the case of Direct Route. So if he is being ridden along with two furlongs to travel, the chances are that he won't win. Conversely, if you see Richard Johnson sitting with a double handful approaching the last, all the better. Toto Toscato is a novice chaser very much to follow.

POINTS TO NOTE
Probable Best Distance   -   2 miles
Preferred Going   -   Soft
Connection's Comments: "We're really looking forward to seeing him go chasing." Owner's husband, STAN CLARKE.

GOING:	R	W	P	TRACK:	R	W	P
Soft	4	2	1	Left Handed	5	1	3
Gd/Sft	1	0	1	Right	2	1	0
Good	2	0	1	Galloping	1	1	0
				Stiff/Undul.	3	1	1
				Tight	3	0	2

TRIP:	R	W	P		R	W	P
2m	5	2	1	2m 2f	1	0	1
2m 1f	1	0	1				

WAHIBA SANDS

6 b g Pharly (FR) - Lovely Noor (USA) (Fappiano (USA))
OWNER: Mr D.A.JOHNSON
TRAINER: M.C.PIPE. Nicholashayne, Somerset.
CAREER FORM FIGURES: 11230 - 12
CAREER WINS: 1997: Dec LEICESTER Soft NH 2m; ASCOT Gd/Sft NH 2m: 1998: Nov NEWBURY Soft HH 2m

"I bought him to go over fences. He looks an out and out chaser, a lovely big son of Pharly," stated Martin Pipe after he had paid 105,000gns at the Doncaster August Sales last year for the ex-John Dunlop trained six year old.

Despite only having two races for his new connections last season, Wahiba Sands still achieved a hurdles rating of 139 which must bode well for his career over fences. He was given a super ride by Richard Dunwoody on his seasonal debut at Newbury in the Grade 2 Gerry Feilden Hurdle. Dictating the pace almost from the outset, he stayed on gamely despite a serious error at the second last to beat Decoupage by five lengths. Wahiba Sands did not reappear again until January and again ran a cracking race to finish a length second to Master Beveled, with the pair eighteen lengths clear of Toto Toscato, in a recognised Champion Hurdle trial at Haydock. Unfortunately that was the last time we saw Wahiba Sands owing to a slight training setback but he is rated a very exciting prospect for novice chasing this season.

It is worth noting owner David Johnson's comments; "He seems a horse who doesn't like too many races." Bearing this in mind, he should be noted when running fresh (4/5 weeks).

POINTS TO NOTE
Probable Best Distance   -   2 miles
Preferred Going   -   Soft
Connection's Comments: "I think he'll be a top class novice chaser." Owner, D. JOHNSON.

GOING:	R	W	P	TRACK:	R	W	P
Soft	3	2	1	Left Handed	4	1	2
Gd/Sft	1	1	0	Right	3	2	1
Good	2	0	1	Galloping	3	2	1
Gd/Fm	1	0	1	Stiff/Undul.	2	1	0
				Tight	2	0	2

TRIP:	R	W	P
2m	7	3	3

WINSTON RUN

7 ch g Derrylin - Craftsmans Made (Jimsun)
OWNER: Mr & Mrs JOHN POYNTON
TRAINER: I.P.WILLIAMS. Alvechurch, Worcestershire.
CAREER FORM FIGURES: 3 - 12 - 34133
CAREER WINS: 1997: Nov SANDOWN Good NHF 2m: 1998: Dec CHEPSTOW Heavy NH 2½ m

Winston Run illustrated what tremendous ability he has when finishing nine and a half lengths third to Barton in the Royal & Sun Alliance Hurdle at Cheltenham last March. His trainer Ian Williams stated afterwards: "He needs a fence and I hope we shall be able to bring him back next year for the chasing equivalent."

Earlier in the season, Winston Run had run two very respectable races behind Mimosa at Cheltenham in October and Rio's King at Chepstow nearly a month later. However, he got off the mark for the season by beating Storm Castle by four lengths in desperate ground, again at the Welsh venue. The seven year old looked a real stayer that day and that will surely hold him in good stead for when he goes chasing. He may have appeared disappointing next time at Ascot when beaten eleven lengths by Magic Combination but his trainer believes the slow early pace was the cause of his downfall.

As his form figures suggest, Winston Run is a most consistent horse and Ian Williams has always believed that we wouldn't see the best of him until he went over fences. He is likely to prove even more effective when stepped up to three miles.

POINTS TO NOTE
Probable Best Distance   -   3 miles
Preferred Going   -   Soft
Connection's Comments: "We have got very high hopes for him over fences." I.WILLIAMS

GOING:	R	W	P	TRACK:	R	W	P
Heavy	1	1	0	Left Handed	5	1	3
Soft	1	0	1	Right	3	1	2
Gd/Sft	3	0	2	Galloping	2	1	1
Good	3	1	2	Stiff/Undul.	5	1	3
				Tight/Undul.	1	0	1

TRIP:	R	W	P		R	W	P
2m	2	1	1	2m 4f	3	1	1
2m 2f	1	0	1	2m 5f	2	0	2

WOODFIELD GALE (IRE)
6 b g Strong Gale - Excitable Lady (Buckskin (FR))
OWNER: Mrs M.B.SCHOLEY
TRAINER: Mrs G.R.REVELEY. Lingdale, Cleveland.
CAREER FORM FIGURES: 43492 - 311120
CAREER WINS: 1998: Oct WETHERBY Soft MH 2m 4f; Nov NEWCASTLE Good HH 2½ m; Dec NEWCASTLE Soft HH 2½ m

Mary Reveley has never been one to rush her horses and she has always thought a great deal of this son of Strong Gale. Having shown promise in bumpers two seasons ago (finished fourth to Muskhill and Barton at Bangor in October 1997), he really got his act together over hurdles last term, winning on three occasions.

Firstly, he accounted for Castletown Count by eleven lengths at Wetherby. Secondly, Joe Buzz by a neck at Newcastle and, thirdly, Grooving by six lengths, also at Gosforth Park. However, arguably Woodfield Gale's two finest performances came in defeat. He was only one and three quarter lengths behind the high-class In Question (trained at the time by Chris Thornton) at Kelso on his seasonal debut in October and was beaten just two and a half lengths by Nicky Henderson's useful novice All Gong at Doncaster in January. The six year old was, admittedly, disappointing on his final start when last of the eleven runners in the Grade 3 EBF Novices' Handicap Hurdle Final at Sandown in March, but I feel that was due to the fact he had been on the go since the Autumn and, significantly, he was retired for the season shortly afterwards.

The fact Woodfield Gale achieved a handicap rating over hurdles of 123 was an excellent achievement, particularly as he is very much a chaser in the making. He should have no trouble with the transition to fences and, according to connections, he does go well fresh so he looks one to note on his novice chasing debut.

POINTS TO NOTE

Probable Best Distance	-	2½ miles
Preferred Going	-	Good

Connection's Comments: "He's always best fresh but he's not the most robust horse and will only get better with age." Mrs M.REVELEY

GOING:	R	W	P	TRACK:	R	W	P
Heavy	1	0	1	Left Handed	8	3	2
Soft	3	2	0	Right	3	0	2
Gd/Sft	3	0	2	Galloping	6	2	1
Good	3	1	1	Tight	4	1	2
Gd/Fm	1	0	0	Tight/Undul.	1	0	1

TRIP:	R	W	P		R	W	P
2m	4	0	2	2m 2f	1	0	1
2m 1f	1	0	0	2m 4f	5	3	1

YOUNG DEVEREAUX (IRE)
6 b or br g Lord Americo - Miss Iverk (Torus)
OWNER: Mr P.K.BARBER, Mr M.COBURN & Mr C.LEWIS
TRAINER: P.F.NICHOLLS. Ditcheat, Somerset.
CAREER FORM FIGURES: 45 - 31
CAREER WIN: 1998: Dec CHEPSTOW Good MH 2m

In his short training career, Paul Nicholls has built up a formidable string of horses and, while the likes of See More Business and Call Equiname captured the headlines last season, unquestionably one of his most exciting prospects for this term is the novice chaser Young Devereaux.

Bought for 26,000gns 'on spec' at the 1998 Doncaster Spring Sales, Young Devereaux was previously in the care of M.Butler in Ireland for whom he ran twice. Injury, unfortunately, meant we only saw him run, also, just twice for Nicholls last season but it was more than enough to suggest he has a decent future, particularly when sent chasing.

A rangy gelding with plenty of scope, Young Devereaux had both his starts last year at Chepstow. Firstly, he ran a smashing race to finish one and a quarter lengths and a neck third to Rio's King in November, having taken the lead at the seventh only to be headed just after the last flight. Secondly, he never looked in the slightest danger in beating Darien and eleven other opponents by upwards of eleven lengths.

How far Young Devereaux will stay is difficult to gauge but he possesses enough speed for two miles, as he showed at Chepstow, and he is a high class novice chaser in the making.

POINTS TO NOTE

Probable Best Distance	-	2 - 2½ miles
Preferred Going	-	Good / Soft

Connection's Comments: **"A lovely horse who has it all ahead of him when it comes to novice chasing this season."** P.NICHOLLS

GOING:	R	W	P	TRACK:	R	W	P
Sft/Hvy	2	0	0	Left Handed	4	1	1
Gd/Sft	1	0	1	Galloping	2	0	0
Good	1	1	0	Stiff/Undul.	2	1	1

TRIP:	R	W	P		R	W	P
2m	1	1	0	2m 3f	1	0	0
2m 2f	1	0	0	2m 4f	1	0	1

YOUNG KENNY
8 b g Ardross - Deirdres Dream (The Parson)
OWNER: Mr J.G.READ
TRAINER: P.BEAUMONT. Stearsby, North Yorkshire.
CAREER FORM FIGURES: 77561 - 7FU3211183 - 21 - 22412U111
CAREER WINS: 1996: May CARTMEL Soft NH 3¼ m; 1997: Jan LEICESTER Gd/Sft NH 3m; Feb CHEPSTOW Good NH 3m; WETHERBY Heavy NH 3m 1f; Dec KELSO Gd/Sft NC 3m 1f: 1998: Dec M.RASEN Heavy HC 4m 1f: 1999: Feb HAYDOCK Soft HC 3½m; UTTOXETER Gd/Sft HC 4¼ m; Apr AYR Soft HC 4m 1f

Young Kenny was arguably One Jump Ahead's biggest success story last season winning the Lincolnshire, the Midlands and the Scottish Grand National, plus the Greenalls Gold Cup at Haydock. He does, of course, retain his place in this year's edition in the hope that he may add the English Grand National at Aintree next April to his collection.

Following one or two indifferent runs at the start of last season, Young Kenny appeared to improve dramatically after the turn of the year. His improvement coincided with a step up in distance. After unfortunately unseating Brian Storey at the first in the Eider Chase at Newcastle, he ran his rivals ragged in the Greenalls Gold Cup beating the consistent mare Fiddling The Facts by thirteen lengths. He then accounted for Call It A Day by eight lengths at Uttoxeter and then he produced a magnificent front running display to land the Scottish National by nine lengths under the welter burden of eleven stone ten. His big race jockey Brendan Powell said afterwards:

"I have no doubts in saying that he's the best staying chaser I've ever ridden, a class horse who can only get better. He's the finished article physically, but mentally he's still a big baby."

A tremendous jumper, Young Kenny looks tailormade for the Grand National and he has to be a major contender for the Welsh equivalent too. The one reservation as regards Aintree could be the ground as he has shown all his best form with plenty of give. Otherwise, he will take all the beating in the long distance staying handicaps this term.

POINTS TO NOTE
Probable Best Distance - 3½ miles +
Preferred Going - Soft / Heavy
Connection's Comments: "This horse is a class stayer. I hope he has everything you need for the National as he jumps well, stays well and copes with big fields. But he must have cut in the ground." P.BEAUMONT

GOING:	R	W	P	TRACK:	R	W	P
Heavy	4	2	1	Left Handed	17	7	4
Soft	5	3	1	Right	9	2	3
Gd/Sft	5	3	1	Galloping	7	2	2
Good	9	1	4	Stiff/Undul.	8	2	4
Gd/Fm	3	0	0	Tight	6	2	1
				Tight/Undul.	5	3	0

TRIP:	R	W	P		R	W	P
2m	1	0	0	3m 1f	6	2	3
2m 1f	1	0	0	3m 2f	3	1	1
2m 4f	1	0	0	3m 4f	1	1	0
2m 7f	1	0	0	4m 1f	3	2	0
3m	8	2	3	4m 2f	1	1	0

TALKING TRAINERS

TIM EASTERBY
Stables: Habton Grange, Great Habton, Malton, North Yorkshire.
1998/99: 28 Winners from 186 Runners 15% Prize-Money £299,043
First-Time Out Winners: 5 11%
Hurdles & NH Flat: 17/124 14% Chases: 11/62 18%

TRACKS TO NOTE (Records from 1994/5 Season +):
AYR 7/20 35%: AINTREE 6/20 30%: CATTERICK 13/55 24%: DONCASTER 8/35 23%:
HEXHAM 4/18 22%: WETHERBY 32/150 21%.

TRAINER'S TIP FOR 1999/2000
SKILLWISE 7 b g Buckley - Calametta
Is back in work now and he will be aimed at three mile novice chases. He jumps like a buck and I am still very hopeful that he will make a good chaser. He had a six-inch gash inside his hock after he ran at Carlisle last season and that is why he only ran once.

BAKKAR (IRE) 5 b g Darshaan - Bayyasa (IRE)
He is currently in Ireland but the intention is for him to come back and he will be running again during the Winter. Only a small horse but he is as game as a pebble and he is a great lepper. He will stay over hurdles and two and a half miles is probably his ideal trip. It is very important that he has fast ground.

BARNBURGH BOY 5 ch g Shalford (IRE) - Tuxford Hideaway
Has been a cracking servant who did tremendously well last season winning five races. Like Bakkar, he is in Ireland at present but he will also be returning. While he goes on most types of ground, he is a much better horse on fast ground. Two miles is his trip.

BARTON 6 ch g Port Etienne (FR) - Peanuts (FR)
As everybody knows, he had a fantastic year last season. As soon as he arrived, we knew he was a good horse as we had trouble finding something to work with him. He is one of those unique horses who certainly has the potential to be a Gold Cup contender one day, with a bit of luck. As for this season, we have not yet decided whether to stay hurdling or go novice chasing. The plan is to run him in the Fighting Fifth Hurdle at Newcastle and then we will make a decision. He has yet to be schooled over fences. I have no doubt that he has the speed for two miles and he will also stay three and a half miles, if necessary. He goes on any ground but, I personally, think he is better on good ground. A lot of people felt he was possibly over the top at Aintree but I can tell you he was 100%. Lorcan (Wyer), quite rightly, rode him confidently, but the others just caught him out for a stride or two after the second last.

BOOGY WOOGY 3 ch g Rock Hopper - Primulette
I think he will make a nice juvenile hurdler this season. His second dam was a high class hurdler so he has the breeding for it. Loves soft ground.

CUMBRIAN CHALLENGE (IRE) 10 ch g Be My Native (USA) - Sixpenny
Has been a wonderful horse for us over the years. He loves Wetherby and Ascot and we will run him in any race at those venues that the BHB Race Planners allow us. He is rated so high now and there just aren't the races for him. The Castleford Chase would have to be high on his agenda again. Two miles is his best trip and he appears to go on any ground, except heavy.

CUMBRIAN MAESTRO 6 b g Puissance - Flicker Toa Flame (USA)
Will go novice chasing this season and I am expecting him to make a nice chaser. He just took a couple of runs to get back to his best last season but I was happy with the progress he made overall. He wouldn't want the ground too firm and I see no reason why he shouldn't stay two and a half miles.

GOOD VIBES 7 b g Ardross - Harmoney Jane
He won't be back until after Christmas. He ran well on his chasing debut at Market Rasen finishing second but he pulled muscles in his back shortly afterwards. When we got that sorted out, he then injured his tendon and it all depends now how it stands up to training. If he makes a full recovery, then he will go straight novice chasing again. He is likely to start off over two miles but he has no problem staying two and a half.

JACKSON PARK 6 gr g Domynsky - Hysteria
He is another who had a problem with a tendon but he is back in work now and the intention is to send him novice chasing. We did actually school him over fences last year and he jumped well. Goes on any ground.

JUSTICE PREVAILED 5 b g Sula Bula - Enchanted Cross
We have always liked him and he ran very well first time out at Newcastle on his debut but he then disappointed at Hexham. By Sula Bula, he is a real good jumper and he looks a nice horse in the making. He has the speed for two miles.

JUST TOM 4 ch g Primitive Rising (USA) - Edenburt
A nice horse who was trained last season by Micky Hammond. He ran well in bumpers and I think he could be alright over hurdles this season. By a sire I like, Primitive Rising, he jumps well at home. A very active horse.

MIXSTERTHETRIXSTER (USA) 3 b g Alleged (USA) - Parliament House (USA)
Was a very good two year old last season but he has proved a bit disappointing this year. We have gelded him and there is every chance that he will go jumping, as we are discussing it at the moment with the owner. If he takes to jumping, he could be a very useful juvenile hurdler.

MONARCH'S PURSUIT 5 b g Pursuit of Love - Last Detail
Goes novice chasing and he could be very good. He is a big horse who has been given plenty of time to develop. A very decent juvenile hurdler two seasons ago, he was very high in the handicap last year so we let him develop as he was still quite weak. He also had a slight sinus problem earlier in his career but that has been cleared up. Two miles is his trip at the moment.

PANAMA HOUSE 4 ch g Rudimentary (USA) - Lustrous
A half brother to Shining Edge, he will be going back over hurdles and I think he will win races. Handicap hurdles over two miles on good fast ground would be ideal.

SCOTTIE YORK 3 b g Noble Patriarch - Devon Dancer
We gave him a run on the Flat at Ripon in July but we think he could make a nice jumper. It is likely that we will give him another run on the Flat. He is a horse we bred ourselves.

SCOTTON GREEN 8 ch g Ardross - Grange Hill Girl
A very tough horse who did well last season winning a couple of races. He had just gone over the top for the year on his last run. Three miles plus is his trip and we are hoping he might develop into a Scottish National contender. Good ground or softer suits him fine.

SHARE OPTIONS (IRE) 8 b or br g Executive Perk - Shannon Belle
A grand horse who jumps for fun. We are, in fact, hoping he could even make a National horse this year. The fences round Aintree wouldn't hold any fears for him. He is a real nice staying chaser who ought to win more races this season. Likes good or softer ground.

SILLY MONEY 8 b g Silly Prices - Playagain
A nice horse who will go back chasing. He was unlucky not to win at Wetherby last season when falling at the third last. He pulled some muscles and then lost his confidence a little. On his day, he is not a bad horse with two miles being his trip.

SIMPLE TONIC 4 gr g Simply Great (FR) - Buck Up
A very nice horse who will make a good novice hurdler this season. He ran in two bumpers last season and he did his job well and so we gave him time to develop. I could see him running in some of those National Hunt novices' hurdles at places like Wetherby. He will start off over two miles but he will stay further.

SIMPLY DASHING (IRE) 8 br g Simply Great (FR) - Qurrat Al Ain
Was unlucky last year not to win a decent race. We made a fatal mistake by running him in the Gold Cup. There were big doubts over whether he would stay and he clearly didn't. When he came back from Cheltenham it was as though he had had three races, he was absolutely knackered. That finished him for the year. What we should have done was run him at Aintree and missed Cheltenham altogether. We will probably stick to two and a half miles this season, although the King George would be a possibility if he gets good or faster ground. He must have decent ground.

SIMPLY GIFTED 4 b g Simply Great (FR) - Souveniers
Had a long season last year and got slightly jarred up at Aintree so we have decided to give him a long rest and he will not be back until after Christmas. There is a possibility that he will go novice chasing in the New Year as he would get the five year old allowances. Otherwise, he will run in some of the good handicap hurdles in the Spring and then go chasing the following season. He is a horse with a lot of natural ability and he will make a lovely chaser.

Unnamed 4 b g Perpendicular - Politique (Politico)
I bought him at the Doncaster Sales in May and he looks a nice horse. We haven't done a lot with him but he ought to be running in a bumper by Christmas time.

JIMMY FITZGERALD

Stables: Norton Grange, Norton, Malton, North Yorkshire.
1998/99: 17 Winners from 152 Runners 11% Prize-Money £85,577
First-Time Out Winners: 5 14%
Hurdles & NH Flat: 11/101 11% Chases: 6/51 12%

TRACKS TO NOTE (Records from 1994/5 Season +):
PERTH 7/19 37%: KELSO 7/23 30%: AYR 4/15 27%: SANDOWN 2/9 22%: CARLISLE 6/29
21%: SEDGEFIELD 12/56 21%

TRAINER'S TIP FOR 1999/2000
MINUIT NOIR (IRE) 3 b g Machiavellian (IRE) - Misbegotten (IRE)
Has run well on the Flat during the Summer, finishing second at York and then winning his
maiden at Pontefract. I think he will make a good juvenile hurdler as he is the sort of horse who
will keep improving as the year goes on. A very laid back horse, he is likely to start off at one of
the better tracks such as Wetherby.

ALZULU (IRE) 8 b g Alzao (USA) - Congress Lady
Is 100% again and he will be going novice chasing this season. He has had trouble with his back
and his joints in the past but I am sure he still retains plenty of ability. Two miles is his trip with
good to soft probably his ideal ground.

BACCARAT (IRE) 5 b g Bob Back (USA) - Sarahlee
Ran well in his bumpers last season and will now go novice hurdling. However, he is very much
a chasing type and there is every chance that he may go over fences after Christmas. I would
expect two and a half miles to prove his best distance.

BALLAD MINSTREL (IRE) 7 gr g Ballad Rock - Sashi Woo
Remains in training with us, despite the very sad death of his owner Edward Shouler. He ran
some good races last season and he will be aimed at two and a half mile handicap chases this
time. Likes soft ground and I will be disappointed if he doesn't win a few more this season.

BLUE BUD 5 b g Lord Bud - Hodsock Venture
Will go novice hurdling and he could be alright. We have schooled him at home and he jumps
very well. The way he races suggests that he will stay well and I can see him winning races over
two and a half to three miles.

DAMBUSTERS 5 b g Damister (USA) - Key To The River (USA)
Another horse who ran in a bumper last season. It was quite a warm contest at Wetherby and he
ran well, especially as he wouldn't have been fully wound up. We will give him another run in a
bumper and then go novice hurdling later in the season. Has plenty of speed and will stick to
two miles for the time being.

HOUSE CAPTAIN 10 br g Oats - Super Princess
Will run in the decent three mile handicap chases. He ran very well in the Royal & Sun Alliance
Chase at Cheltenham but Graham Bradley felt he would have been placed had he been 100%
right. When he came back, we found a chip in his joint. He is OK now and I think he will win a

good handicap this season. Something like the Hennessy could be a possibility. He does like good ground.

ILAHABAD (IRE) 4 b g Kahyasi - Ilmiyya (FR)
Belongs to Sir Peter O'Sullevan and he will be running in handicap hurdles. Everyone who has ridden him says he will stay two and a half miles so we will step him up in trip. He is not really big enough to jump fences.

JUSTIN MAC (IRE) 8 br g Satco (FR) - Quantas
Goes novice chasing. He started last season off very well winning at Kelso but he proved disappointing overall. However, I don't think he was quite right in the second half of the season. He is looking well at present and has schooled well over fences. Two miles is his trip.

LAST HAVEN (FR) 3 b g Slip Anchor - Lady Norcliffe (USA)
He won as a two year old at Pontefract and is a half brother to Paul Nicholls' Norski Lad, who won four races last season. We will probably give him another run or two on the Flat but his real job will be juvenile hurdling. Although we have yet to school him, I don't see him having any problems.

MUNDO RARO 4 b g Zafonic (USA) - Star Spectacle
We have schooled him over jumps and he goes novice hurdling. I am expecting him to make up into a decent novice as he has shown some good form on the Flat. Despite being by Zafonic, he will have no trouble staying two miles and he does like fast ground.

PHAR SMOOTHER (IRE) 7 br g Phardante (FR) - Loughaderra
Was running a good race on his chasing debut at Wetherby last season when he fell down the back straight. Unfortunately, he then twisted a gut and he had to be operated on. He is fine now and will go back over fences this season. He came back into work quite early and should be running by the Autumn. Two and a half miles on good ground are his conditions.

REQUESTOR 4 b g Distinctly North (USA) - Bebe Altesse (GER)
He is another horse owned by the Marquesa who will be going jumping for the first time. He ran a good race on the Flat at York in July and he has the making of a nice hurdler. Two miles will be his trip.

SYMONDS INN 5 ch g In The Wings - Shining Eyes (USA)
We have given him the Summer off and he will be campaigned in handicap hurdles over three miles. He has also been gelded since last season. Likes soft ground and he ought to win again this season.

WESTERTON (IRE) 6 b g Glacial Storm (USA) - Killiney Rose
Was very consistent last season winning at Sedgefield and Uttoxeter. You can forget his last run as he was suffering with the virus. Loves soft ground and he will go straight over fences this year. We will probably start him off over two and a half miles but he will stay three alright.

WHIP HAND (IRE) 8 br g Bob Back (USA) - Praise The Lord
Won his first novice chase at Market Rasen last season and then finished second at Newbury.

However, we found that he had a touch of a leg afterwards so, rather than risk him, we gave him the rest of the season off. He will come back into work in October and, hopefully, will be running soon after Christmas. On his form last season, he wouldn't have been far behind the best two mile novice chasers. Two miles is ideal.

Unnamed 4 b g Phardante (FR) - Don't Be Late
A lovely big horse who we plan to start off in bumpers. We haven't done an awful lot with him yet but he looks a nice horse.

Unnamed 4 ch g Minster Son - Sister Claire
He is another nice big horse we are likely to start off in bumpers. We broke him in during the Summer so it is early days to say how good he could be.

RISING STAR FOR THE NEW MILLENNIUM

CHRIS GRANT
Stables: Low Burntoft Farm, Wolviston, Billingham, Cleveland.
1998/99: 17 Winners from 132 Runners 13% Prize-Money £83,009
First-Time Out Winners: 1 3%
Hurdles & NH Flat: 11/88 13% Chases: 6/44 14%

TRACKS TO NOTE (Records from 1994/5 Season +):
MUSSELBURGH 3/14 21%

TRAINER'S TIP FOR 1999/2000

SIKANDER A AZAM 6 b g Arctic Lord - Shanlaragh
Will go novice chasing and I am hoping he could be very good. He is a free running sort who likes good ground. While we have yet to school him officially, he did jump a fence at Doncaster the wrong way round one day when he got loose going to the start. I suppose if he can jump a fence the wrong way then I am sure he can jump one going the right way ! Two miles is his trip.

BIROTEX BOY (IRE) 6 b g Meneval (USA) - Ballymorris Belle
Had a slight hiccup last year and it was enough for him to miss the whole of the season. He is 100% now and we are going to send him novice chasing. He was placed over hurdles the season before but he has the physique of a chaser. We will probably start him off over two and a half miles and I would say good to soft ground suits him best.

BREATH OF SCANDAL (IRE) 8 br g Strong Gale - Her Name Was Lola
Won two novice chases for us last season and he is a horse with a fair amount of ability. He is a free running sort and we are hoping he will make up into a useful staying handicapper this year.While he wouldn't want heavy ground, he certain wants it on the easy side of good.

CHASING BAILEY'S 5 b g Neltino - Rosie Oh
We gave him two runs last term and he looks a nice type of horse. The intention is to start him off in novice hurdles but we may send him chasing after Christmas. He was still a bit weak last year but he has done well over the Summer. Two and a half miles will be his trip to begin with.

HUNTING SLANE 7 b g Move Off - Singing Slane
Did very well last season winning five races. A very tough and genuine horse, we are going to send him novice chasing. He is not very big but he does jump well. He is a versatile horse having won over two and a quarter miles and three miles one and he appears to be well suited by the sharper tracks. Provided they go a good gallop and there is plenty of pace then he will always run his race.

MASTER WOOD 8 b g Wonderful Surprise - Miss Wood
Another super horse who did well last season winning three. He is owned by Roy Robinson who used to train. Likes a stiff track and I am hoping he can win a few more staying handicaps around the Northern tracks. He likes the ground on the easy side.

ROI DE LA CHASSE 6 ch g Royal Vulcan - Hunt The Thimble (FR)
A very consistent horse who improved as the season went on. He ended the year by finishing a good fourth in that decent novices' handicap at Sandown behind some useful horses. A big chasing type, I am hoping he will make a nice novice chaser this season. He was still relatively weak last year but he has really strengthened up during the Summer.

SHERMI (IRE) 5 b g Beau Sher - Woodland Theory
Was very weak and immature last season when he ran in a couple of bumpers and hurdles. I have been pleased with him during the Summer and the plan is for him to go straight over fences. We will start him off over two and a half but three miles won't be a problem later on.

NICKY HENDERSON
Stables: Seven Barrows, Lambourn, Berkshire.
1998/99: 73 Winners from 315 Runners 23% Prize-Money £584,007
First-Time Out Winners: 24 26%
Hurdles & NH Flat: 52/200 26% Chases: 21/115 18%

TRACKS TO NOTE (Records from 1994/5 Season +):
LUDLOW 13/33 39%: PLUMPTON 9/24 38%: FOLKESTONE 10/28 36%: HEREFORD 9/27 33%: TAUNTON 9/27 33%: DONCASTER 11/36 31%: NEWTON ABBOT 4/14 29%: HUNTINGDON 12/46 26%: STRATFORD 8/35 23%.

TRAINER'S TIP FOR 1999/2000
BLUE ROYAL (FR) 4 b g Dauphin du Bourg (FR) - Before The Flag (IRE)
I am hoping he will be very good. He was unlucky not to win first time out for us at Sandown but, as it turned out, it helped us as he was eligible for the 'winners of one' at Punchestown, which of course he won. I thought he was very impressive at Punchestown. There is not quite the same incentive now to go over fences so soon as the allowances for five year olds have changed. I would think we will see how far we can go over hurdles before we start considering chasing. He is, however, a huge horse and is very much a chaser in the making.

ADMIRAL ROSE 5 b g Handsome Sailor - Rose Ravine
I was pleased with him last year. He won the second of his two bumpers at Chepstow and he comes from a good family. The plan is for him to now go novice hurdling and being out of a staying mare, I would expect him to stay well.

ARTEMIS (IRE) 7 b g Strong Gale - Ethel's Daughter
He is quite a nice horse and the plan is for him to go novice chasing this season. Two and a half miles plus would be his trip.

BACCHANAL (IRE) 5 ch g Bob Back (USA) - Justitia
Is a lovely horse and I am hoping he will turn out to be very good. He was unlucky at Punchestown as he came back with a slight injury. It was such a pity as it would have told us how good he is. Back in work now, he has done plenty of walking. He is a proper National Hunt horse and it is likely that we will send him novice chasing. We will start him off at two miles but I have no doubts that he will stay further. Loves soft ground.

BE BRAVE (FR) 6 b m Green Forest (USA) - Belle Brava (USA)
She is a mare I have always thought a lot of but she only ran once last season. We are going to send her novice chasing as she is an excellent jumper.

BORO SOVEREIGN (IRE) 6 b g King's Ride - Boro Penny
Won his bumper and then threw away a race at Wincanton. He then went to Newbury but returned with a slight pelvic problem. He is OK now and will go straight over fences. We will probably start him off over two and a half, although he will stay further. He should make a nice chaser.

BRANDY SNAP 5 ch m Broadsword (USA) - Brand
She is a bit like Admiral Rose, in that she has had a couple of bumpers and has done nothing wrong. She is a strong home-bred mare who will go novice hurdling and I am expecting her to stay well, being by Broadsword.

CAPTAIN LEAU (FR) 4 b g Ganges (USA) - Disco Dancer
A lovely horse who has come from France where he ran in a number of decent hurdles at Auteuil. He will go novice hurdling and is very much one to look forward to.

CEANANNAS MOR (IRE) 5 b or br g Strong Gale - Game Sunset
He is a full brother to Stormyfairweather and he looks a lovely horse. He won his only point to point in Ireland last April and I am certainly looking forward to training him.

CLASSY LAD (NZ) 9 b or br g Golden Elder - Barrel (NZ)
Missed last season but he is back now and he will be aimed at two mile handicap chases. A couple of years ago, he wasn't that far behind the best two mile novices. Likes good ground.

DUSK DUEL (USA) 4 b g Kris - Night Secret
A good horse who won first time out at Sandown. Everything went wrong for him next time at Aintree. He went very wide turning into the straight and never got into the race. Flat bred, he has plenty of speed and two miles will be his trip over hurdles.

EASTER ROSS 6 ch g Ardross - Caserta
Will definitely go novice chasing and I am hoping he could be very good. The most disappointing aspect for him last season was Cheltenham when he fell early on. It was a tragedy. He was still a big baby last year but he has Summered very well and I am looking forward to him over fences. He must have good ground.

ESPRIT DE COTTE (FR) 7 b g Lute Antique (FR) - Rafale de Cotte (FR)

Looked good when winning at Stratford but you have got to say it was a bad race. The main purpose of running there was to try and get him handicapped. He did win a chase in France so, if we decide to go over fences, then he must go straight into handicaps. Depending on what the handicapper decides to do with him, we may just try and exploit his mark over hurdles before going chasing. I do think he is a bloody nice horse who stays well.

FAR HORIZON (IRE) 5 b g Phardante (FR) - Polly Puttens

A nice horse with a lot of quality. He was very impressive when winning his bumper but it wouldn't have been the strongest of races. I am hoping he will be very good. He will go straight over hurdles now and will start off over two miles.

FATHER MANSFIELD (IRE) 5 b g Phardante (FR) - Lena's Reign

I like him a lot. We bought him at the Doncaster Spring Sales after he had won a couple of Irish point to points. I honestly don't know what we will do with him yet but you would think he will start off in a novice hurdle and we will take it from there.

FIDDLING THE FACTS (IRE) 8 b or br m Orchestra - Facts 'n Fancies

She is back in work and she is looking huge. Obviously the plan is the Grand National again and you would have to say races such as the Welsh National will be other targets along the way. She was running a super race in the National last year and she appeared to be loving it. She jumped brilliantly and what it did tell us was that soft ground is not essential for her.

GAROLSA (FR) 5 b g Rivelago (FR) - Rols du Chatelier (FR)

I am hoping he is a nice horse. He came from France and we gave him time to acclimatise before he won his only start last year at Chepstow. I was pleased with him that day and the plan is to send him novice chasing.

GET REAL (IRE) 8 br g Executive Perk - Lisa's Music

Ran an excellent race in the Victor Chandler Chase and, as it turned out, he came up against the Queen Mother winner. In many ways, I think he was unlucky as he would have preferred the race to be run at Ascot, where it was originally planned for, as it would have suited him better than Kempton. Unfortunately, he picked up an injury at Kempton and he missed the rest of the year. He will run in all the top two mile chases he can, although he must go right handed. You are very unlikely to see him going left handed again. Punchestown would be a possibility towards the end of the season.

GRECIAN DART (IRE) 7 b g Darshaan - Grecian Urn

Goes novice chasing and he could be very good. Mick (Fitzgerald) thinks he will jump fences alright and he had some good hurdles form last season. Two miles is his trip at the moment but I'm sure he'll get two and a half. Likes good ground.

HELIETTE (FR) 4 b f Tropular - Fraulein (FR)

She looks a nice filly and she is actually for sale. She had some good form on the Flat in France last year and we gave her plenty of time to acclimatise. Has plenty of pace and she looks as though she will want some cut in the ground.

HIDEBOUND (IRE) 7 b g Buckskin (FR) - Merry Run
Had a slight problem with his knee last season but he is back in work now and he is a seriously good horse. The plan is for him to go novice chasing and I am hoping he will turn out to be very good. Loves soft ground.

IBOGA (FR) 3 b f Cyborg (FR) - Quintessence III (FR)
She is a filly who is a full sister to Cyborgo and Hors La Loi. I would imagine we will send her juvenile hurdling, although bumpers after Christmas is another option.

KATARINO (FR) 4 b g Pistolet Bleu (IRE) - Katevana (FR)
He, of course, had a fantastic year last season and there is every chance that he will go to France in October for a hurdle race. At that time of the year, the ground is much more likely to be soft in France than it is over here. He would only go for the Champion Hurdle if the ground was soft and it may turn out that he will develop into a Stayers' Hurdle candidate. I would think it is highly unlikely that he will go chasing this season.

KINGS BOY (IRE) 5 ch g Be My Native (USA) - Love-In-A-Mist
I wouldn't really know what to make of him. He is the most laid back horse I think I have come across. There is every chance that we may send him novice chasing. While he is still quite a backward horse, he has done very well physically over the Summer and is very much a chasing type of horse. He goes on any ground. A very nice horse.

KINGS RAPID (IRE) 5 b g King's Ride - Smokey River
He has yet to run but he looks a nice horse at home and he has done everything we have asked of him. We have done a fair bit with him but his owner, Mr Hemmings, is very patient. He is a big horse and I would imagine he will start off in a bumper.

LONG LUNCH (IRE) 7 b g Executive Perk - Bell Walks Rose
He is quite a nice horse who won his only start last season. The ground was plenty quick enough for him that day and he picked up a slight injury so we gave him the rest of the season off. He will go straight over hurdles this year.

MAGIC CIRCLE (FR) 7 b g Bering - Lucky Round
He is a huge horse and we sent him to Sandown one day last season thinking it would suit him but unfortunately he came back with a chip in his knee. He is OK again now and he will go novice chasing. We may start him off over two miles but I'm sure he will get further.

MAKOUNJI (FR) 5 b m Tip Moss (FR) - Maisonnaise (FR)
Had a fantastic season last year and we are hoping she can go on from there. However, she is going to find it much tougher as she won't receive as many allowances now. She was badly in season at Cheltenham and she patently did not stay at Aintree, although she had probably had enough for the season by then. You would think two and a half miles would be her best trip.

MASAMADAS 4 ch g Elmaamul (USA) - Beau's Delight (USA)
He has done very well over the Summer and he needed to. He has had a nice long break having been on the go for a while and the plan is to aim him at two mile handicap hurdles. Likes good ground.

OBELISK (IRE) 5 b g Alzao (USA) - Obertura (USA)
A new horse to the yard. He was trained last season by Bill Haigh and he showed good form in bumpers. We have not done anything with him yet so I can't tell you a lot. However, he will be going novice hurdling this season.

PERFECT VENUE (IRE) 6 b g Danehill (USA) - Welsh Fantasy
He is a useful horse on his day. A winner of two races last season, he will be aimed at two mile handicap hurdles. Likes soft ground.

PREMIER GENERATION (IRE) 6 b g Cadeaux Genereux - Bristle
Another who had a very good year. We have given him a nice break as he had been running on the Flat this time last year. Two mile handicap hurdles are his target.

REGAL GALE (IRE) 5 b g Strong Gale - Dikler's Queen (IRE)
A very, very big horse who has yet to run. We haven't done a great deal with him but I do like him. I would think he will go straight over hurdles.

RUNAWAY BISHOP (USA) 4 b g Lear Fan (USA) - Valid Linda (USA)
We bought him out of Jessica Harrington's yard at the Doncaster Spring Sales. He was placed in three bumpers in Ireland last season and he looks a nice horse. Novice hurdling will be his game this season.

SALMON BREEZE (IRE) 8 ch g Kambalda - Channel Breeze
Did well last season winning two novice chases and he could have won a few more if things had gone his way. He pulled some muscles in his backside towards the end of the season but he looks to be going the right way. He does not want the ground too soft.

SERENUS (USA) 6 b g Sunshine Forever (USA) - Curl And Set (USA)
He has been an absolute star. A very small horse, he was brilliant last year and he even managed to win a race on the Flat in the Spring. He loves Kempton and we are going to try and win a novice chase there. There wouldn't be many horses which have won a Flat race, a hurdle and a chase at the same course. Two miles is his trip, although we may try him over two and a half.

SHARPICAL 7 b g Sharpo - Magical Spirit
Has done very, very well over the Summer. He was wrong after trying to win the Tote Gold Trophy for a second time but we have kept him going during the Summer and he is looking fantastic. We are going to send him novice chasing and he could be very good, indeed. He has a tremendous amount of natural ability.

STEEL BLADE (IRE) 6 gr g Lafontaine (USA) - Steal On
Has joined us from Kim Bailey. As everyone knows, he is a half brother to One Man and I am very much looking forward to training him. We haven't made any plans yet but he is almost certain to go straight over hurdles.

STORMYFAIRWEATHER (IRE) 7 b g Strong Gale - Game Sunset
A star who had a fantastic year last season. He was so brave when winning at Cheltenham and then finishing second at Punchestown. His run in Ireland shows that he stays three miles and that gives us a few more options. He does like good ground.

TAX EXEMPT (IRE) 5 b g Be My Native (USA) - I'll Say She Is
Had one run last season and was impressive. Unfortunately, he picked up a slight injury in the process and we are not quite sure what the handicapper is going to make of his win. If the handicapper allows us then we will start off low key and build our way up. Two miles is his trip for the time being.

TEMPESTUOUS LADY (IRE) 8 b m Sexton Blake - Lady-Easton
On her day she is a very good mare, although she is inclined to throw in the odd stinker like at Aintree last season. She is a great jumper and we are going to send her novice chasing. Three miles is her trip and I think she will make a nice chaser.

TEQUILA 4 b g Mystiko (USA) - Black Ivor (USA)
We have gelded him and I hoping he will improve considerably as a result. He won easily at Wincanton and we sent him to Aintree thinking it would suit him but he didn't run as well as I had hoped. There is definitely more to come and he is a horse with bags of speed. Likes good ground.

TIUTCHEV 6 b g Soviet Star (USA) - Cut Ahead
He has joined us from David Nicholson's. I very much doubt if he will run over hurdles as the plan is to go novice chasing. He had some very good form as a hurdler and could be a top class prospect for chasing over two miles.

VIA DE LA VALLE (IRE) 5 ch g Nearly A Nose - Willabelle
A good looking horse we bought at the Doncaster Spring Sales. He won his point in Ireland and he looks to have a lot of quality. Very active, I would imagine he will start the season off over hurdles.

YOKKI MOPPIE (USA) 5 b m Local Talent (USA) - Hint of Intrigue (CAN)
She looked very good when winning her only start for us since coming from France. She had a slight problem afterwards but she is OK now and she should be out around Christmas time, over hurdles.

PHILIP HOBBS
Stables: Sandhill, Bilbrook, Minehead, Somerset.
1998/99: 84 Winners from 441 Runners 19% Prize-Money £595,766
First-Time Out Winners: 22 19%
Hurdles & NH Flat: 49/302 16% Chases: 35/139 25%

TRACKS TO NOTE (Records from 1994/5 Season +):
PERTH 15/32 47%: HUNTINGDON 8/23 35%: BANGOR 10/36 28%: CHEPSTOW 30/111 27%: NEWTON ABBOT 42/158 27%: TAUNTON 29/120 24%: EXETER 37/158 23%: SANDOWN 13/56 23%.

ANTIQUE GOLD 5 b g Gildoran - Chanelle
A half brother to Country Beau, he ran well in a couple of bumpers last season and he will now go straight over hurdles. We have schooled him and he jumps well and he will probably start off in a two and a half miles novice hurdle in October. Likes cut in the ground.

BOUCHASSON (FR) 6 b g Big John (FR) - Kizil Ayak (FR)
Did amazingly well winning the valuable novices' chase at Ayr and then winning easily at Punchestown. He is now rated 132 and his first main target is the First National Bank Chase at Ascot in November. That race is over two and a half miles but he is going to be better over three. He might just be very good.

CALHOUN (FR) 4 b g Sheyrann - Blanche Dame (FR)
I would like to think he can win a bumper before going novice hurdling. He ought to be on the track by October but he would not want the ground too soft. We will keep him to two miles for the time being.

CELTIC NATIVE (IRE) 4 b or br m Be My Native (USA) - Tarahumara
She is a new horse to the yard having finished a promising second in an Irish point to point in May. We will start her in a mares bumper and then go novice hurdling. Still only four, she looks a nice mare.

CLIFTON BEAT (USA) 8 b g Danzatore (CAN) - Amenity (FR)
Another who is rated 130, he will have to contest some of the better two mile handicap chases. A race such as the Victor Chandler is a distinct possibility later in the season. Good ground suits him best.

DOCTOR GODDARD 4 b g Niniski (USA) - Kamada (USA)
Just had the one run for us last season at Cheltenham in October and he was very unlucky not to win. He made a bad mistake at the third last and then finished with a flourish. Unfortunately, he cracked a bone in his hind leg and he missed the rest of the season. Two miles is his trip and I think he could be a nice horse this year.

DR LEUNT (IRE) 8 ch g Kefaah (USA) - Not Mistaken (USA)
Rated 151, it is borderline whether he runs in handicaps or level weight chases. He is effective over two and a half but stays three miles as he showed by winning the *Racing Post* Chase. It would have to be very soft for him to run in the Murphy's at Cheltenham. The long term plan is the Grand National.

GAI MURMURE (FR) 5 ch g Murmure (FR) - Venus Guichoise (FR)
Ran well on his sole start for us last season at Cheltenham. He pulled some ligaments off his spine and missed the rest of the year but he is OK now and he could be a nice novice hurdler this season. I hope to have him running by October. Very much a chaser in the making.

GOOD LORD MURPHY (IRE) 7 br g Montelimar (USA) - Semiwild (USA)
Was very disappointing as I thought he was going to be our best horse last season. He pulled muscles on his chasing debut at Exeter and, by the time he had recovered, we put him back over hurdles as we didn't want to break his novice status over fences so late in the season. He has a lot of ability and I am still hopeful that he will make a good chaser. Three miles on soft ground are his conditions.

HANDYMAN (IRE) 5 b g Hollow Hand - Shady Ahan
Could be a very nice horse this year. He is a big backward horse who has needed plenty of time.

I think he has got the ability to win a bumper before going novice hurdling. He is likely to want two and a half miles over hurdles.

IN THE BLOOD (IRE) 8 b g Henbit (USA) - Polly's Slipper
A very progressive horse who won four handicap chases last season. Rated 130, he will have to go for some of the better handicaps, although his owner is keen to stick to the smaller tracks. The only time he has run over three miles is when he fell, going well, at Worcester last season but I don't think he will have any trouble staying. His long term target is the Grand National.

KING WIZARD (IRE) 5 b or br g Supreme Leader - Magic User
A big horse who could be very nice over hurdles this season. He won't run in any more bumpers and will want at least two and a half miles over hurdles. I like him.

LEABURN (IRE) 6 b g Tremblant - Conderlea
A lovely horse but he ran badly on his final start at Sandown and I don't know why. He jumps very well and, although he will have a run over hurdles first, he will be going novice chasing this season. Has plenty of speed and will stay at two miles for now.

MAJOR ADVENTURE (IRE) 6 b g Glacial Storm (USA) - Dual Adventure
An ex-Irish pointer, he never ran last season as he pulled ligaments in his back. It was nothing serious and he is OK now. I do like him and I think he will develop into a very nice horse. He will start off in two and a half mile novice hurdles and then go chasing.

MONT ACA (FR) 4 b g Phantom Breeze - Azuzuama (FR)
He is another who didn't run last season, having banged a joint in the swimming pool. His owner has been very patient and he looks a real nice horse. He was placed on the Flat in France and will begin in two mile novice hurdles.

MUSICAL SLING (IRE) 6 b g Orchestra - Coctail Bid
Did well winning a couple of races over hurdles but his future is over fences and that is what he will do this season. A big strong horse, he has schooled well and I am hoping he will make a good novice chaser.

NATIVE ARROW (IRE) 5 ch g Be My Native (USA) - Clover Run (IRE)
Won a bumper at Wincanton on his debut but he was then slightly disappointing. It is possible that he did not like the soft ground he was racing on. He has schooled well over hurdles and will be running in September.

NATIVE FLING (IRE) 7 b g Be My Native (USA) - Queens Romance
Did very well last year winning four races, including one at the Punchestown Festival. He is quite high in the handicap off a mark of 114 but he is improving so I am hopeful that he can defy that.

NORLANDIC (NZ) 7 ch g First Norman (USA) - April Snow (NZ)
Won his two chases very easily last season and he looks to be on the upgrade. We have always liked him a lot and he looks potentially very well handicapped with a rating of 109. Stays well and I am hopeful that he can do as well as In The Blood did last season as Norlandic is on a similar mark to what he was at this stage.

NUVELLINO 4 b g Robellino (USA) - Furry Dance (USA)
Ran well in some very good novice hurdles last season. We thought if he didn't win any then he would still be a novice for this year. He has had a slight problem with his breathing which may have given the impression that he wasn't truly staying the two miles but he has been operated on since. He is a nice horse who should win races this season.

ORSWELL LAD 10 b g Pragmatic - Craftsmans Made
Finished third in the Kim Muir at Cheltenham and he could be aimed at the Grand National this season. He jumped round there in the John Hughes two years ago so the fences won't be a problem. Loves soft ground.

PAPO KHARISMA 9 b g Rakoposhi King - Royal Pam
He had an amazing year last season winning five races including at Aintree in April. We bought him very cheaply at Doncaster and he did remarkably well. He will go novice chasing this season and, having schooled well, I think he will have another good year. We may start him off over two and a half but he really wants three miles.

PHARDANTE FLYER (IRE) 5 b g Phardante (FR) - Shannon Lek
Ran a very promising race at Cheltenham in a bumper but then suffered a minor stress fracture of his pelvis. He is good enough to win a bumper before going novice hurdling. Two and a half miles will suit him.

QUALITY (IRE) 6 b g Rock City - Queens Welcome
Missed the whole of last season but he is fine now and he will be running in handicap hurdles and then he is likely to go novice chasing later on.

ROSS MINSTER (IRE) 5 b or br g Roselier (FR) - Face To Face
An out an out stayer who will be aimed at three mile novice hurdles. Long term, he is very much a chaser in the making. I would like to think he will pick up a race or two over hurdles before then, though.

SADLER'S REALM 6 b g Sadler's Wells (USA) - Rensaler (USA)
Goes novice chasing and he could be very good. A very decent horse on his day, he does like a cut in the ground with two and a half miles being his optimum trip.

SAMLEE (IRE) 10 b g Good Thyne (USA) - Annie Buskins
Broke a blood vessel in last season's Grand National. He still retains plenty of ability and there is definitely another good race to be won with him. In all likelihood, he will be aimed at the National again.

STORMY PASSAGE (IRE) 9 b g Strong Gale - Perusia
A very decent horse but, unfortunately, he breaks blood vessels. I still think he is capable of winning one of the big two and a half mile handicaps so the Murphy's is a definite possibility. He does go very well fresh so we may send him straight there without a race beforehand.

TANTIVY BAY (IRE) 5 b g Good Thyne (USA) - Swiftly Belle
Won his bumper at Towcester very well last season. He had been working nicely at home and

we thought he would win. He appeared to idle in front but won comfortably. Has schooled well at home and we are very hopeful about his future over hurdles. A nice horse.

TEMPER LAD (USA) 4 b g Riverman (USA) - Dokki (USA)
A tiny horse we bought at the 1998 Newmarket Sales and he has done nothing but improve since we have had him. He did have a breathing problem but that was very successfully operated on. Rated 120, he is plenty high enough in the handicap but he is still improving and he will run in some decent handicap hurdles.

THELONIUS (IRE) 4 ch g Statoblest - Little Sega (FR)
We bought him out of Julian Smyth-Osbourne's yard at the 1998 Newmarket Autumn Sales but we never ran him last season as he had been on the go for a while having run and won on the Flat. He is a nice big horse who should make a nice four year old novice hurdler this year.

UPHAM LORD (IRE) 6 b g Lord Americo - Top O The Mall
Ran in staying novice hurdles at some of the better tracks last season without getting his head in front but I think he should be capable of winning a race, at least, before he goes novice chasing.

VILLAGE KING (IRE) 6 b g Roi Danzig (USA) - Honorine (USA)
Enjoyed a fantastic season last year winning five races and finishing second at Aintree. He is now rated 127 but he ought to pay his way. The key to him is the ground, he doesn't want it any softer than good.

Unnamed 4 b g Perpendicular - Stubbin Moor
He is a very nice horse whom we bought at the 1998 Doncaster Spring Sales. He has been working well and the plan is to start him off in a bumper and he could be the sort to win first time out. He will go hurdling later in the season.

LENNY LUNGO
Stables: Hetland Hill Farm, Carrutherstown, Dumfriesshire.
1998/99: 56 Winners from 288 Runners 19% Prize-Money £287,241
First-Time Out Winners: 7 12%
Hurdles & NH Flat: 34/198 17% Chases: 22/90 24%

TRACKS TO NOTE (Records from 1994/5 Season +):
UTTOXETER 5/12 42%: HEXHAM 21/94 22%: PERTH 11/50 22%: SEDGEFIELD 10/49 20%.

TRAINER'S TIP FOR 1999/2000
LORD OF THE SKY 6 b g Lord Bud - Fardella (ITY)
He ran twice for us last season in bumpers and won both times. He was impressive both times and especially so on his second start as he was carrying a penalty. We know he can jump as he won a point to point before he joined us and he looks a horse to be really excited about. He came back from Hexham slightly jarred up so we gave him plenty of time and he is 100% now. We will take our time with him and wait for the right opportunities. I am hoping we can run up a sequence with him and then, depending on his trip, aim him at something like the Hennessy Series which Crazy Horse won the final of last season. If we find he is not quick enough then we

will step him up in trip. He won't have another run in a bumper, though.

BALLYSTONE (IRE) 6 ch g Roselier (FR) - Gusserane Princess
He looks a nice horse who was placed in an Irish point to point. He seems a very tough horse who jumps well. I would think we will start him off in a novice hurdle and then go chasing. Three miles will be his trip.

BIRKDALE (IRE) 8 gr g Roselier (FR) - Clonroche Lady
Did very well over hurdles last season but he has really paid the price as the handicapper put him up an unbelievable amount each time. He is now rated 150 over hurdles and we have nowhere to go with him. It leaves us no option but to go back over fences. He is not a big horse and nor is he very long so when he runs over fences in soft ground, he tends to sink a little and the fences look that little bit bigger for him. The plan is to run him on proper good National Hunt ground. He is very brave and never gives up and he stays forever.

CORSTON JOKER 9 b g Idiot's Delight - Corston Lass
We have problems with him as he realises there is an option as to whether to race or not and he has decided it is far easier not to bother. The plan is to send him hunting and try and sweeten him up. The funny thing is that when he does decide to race he is the most honest horse you could wish to have. He undoubtedly has ability and, while most of his winning has come over two and a half miles, I am sure he will stay three. Good ground suits him as he hates the soft.

CRAZY HORSE (IRE) 6 b g Little Bighorn - Our Dorcet
Had a sensational year last season winning the Hennessy Series at Kelso and finishing third in the Scottish Champion Hurdle. As a result, he is high in the handicap and there are not that many races for him. However, we plan to step him up to two and a half miles this season and see what happens. If we think he has done as much as he can over hurdles by Christmas then we may just give him a school over fences. I would like to think there is another hurdle race in him. He is only a small horse and does not have the ideal stature for chasing. I think the reason why he improved so much after his first two runs over hurdles last season was because he had learnt to settle. Previously he was too keen and was burning himself out and not staying the trip.

DANTE'S GLEN (IRE) 5 ch g Phardante (FR) - Glen Laura
A tall rangy horse who did well to be second in an Irish point as a four year old. He did show some promise over hurdles last season and we may give him another couple of runs before going novice chasing. He is bred to be a chaser and I think he will stay three miles OK.

EVENIN ALL (IRE) 6 b g Dromod Hill - Barna Havna
Took a while to get his act together last season, jumping very carefully and not getting away from his hurdles quickly enough. However, he got better as the season went on and, being from the family of General Crack, he will stay forever. The plan is to have another couple of runs over hurdles before going chasing. Fences should help him as they will go that bit slower.

FLIGHTY LEADER (IRE) 7 b g Supreme Leader - Flighty Ann
Won an Irish point before joining us and was placed last season over hurdles. He is more than capable of winning races and he will begin the year over hurdles. I think he will stay three miles but he wouldn't want the ground too soft.

GLACIAL DANCER (IRE) 6 b g Glacial Storm (USA) - Castleblagh
Ran very well on a number of occasions last season without winning before finally getting his head in front at Hexham. He is a lovely long striding horse who goes on any ground. We won't be keeping him over hurdles much longer as he is very much a chaser in the making. He definitely stays two and a half miles and, on good ground, I don't see why he shouldn't stay three.

LORD OF THE LOCH (IRE) 8 b or br g Lord Americo - Loughamaire
Likes soft ground and produced a tremendous performance to win after a year off at Perth. We were slightly disappointed with him next time as everything seemed to be in his favour. He will remain over hurdles and, being a stayer, three miles suits him well.

MENSHAAR (USA) 7 b g Hawkster (USA) - Klassy Imp (USA)
Very consistent last year, he was hardly out of the frame. A very laid back horse, he is bone idle. He is a clever horse who jumps fences well and he will be aimed at the long distance handicaps at places like Market Rasen and Newcastle.

MIKE STAN (IRE) 8 b g Rontino - Fair Pirouette
Jumps fences well although he may have been a touch fortunate to win at Ayr when he was left clear. He is not very big and we don't have any big targets for him this season. He has won on a wide range of going but I personally think he is better on good ground.

NATIVE AFFAIR (IRE) 5 ch g Be My Native (USA) - Queens Romance
Likes good ground and certainly does not want it soft. He is still a young horse who maybe still improving. We are hoping he will prove good enough to follow a similar programme to Lord of the Sky, with races such as the Hennessy Series being the target. He showed a good turn of foot to win his bumpers so we will start him off over two miles over hurdles.

PADDY MAGUIRE (IRE) 6 b g Mazaad - Knocknagow
Won a point in Ireland and I must say I was a bit disappointed with him last season, although he did run better at Perth last time. He is still a young horse and I am hoping there is more improvement to come. We will try and win a novice handicap with him over hurdles before going chasing. Three miles on good ground would be his conditions.

PHAR ECHO (IRE) 8 b g Phardante (FR) - Borecca
Won two hurdles races last season and we will follow a similar programme this year, alternating between hurdles and fences. While he is no star, he always wins a couple each season. Three miles is his trip.

RED HOT INDIAN (IRE) 6 b g Little Bighorn - Pepper Cannister
Was disappointing last season. He had won his bumper the previous year and I thought he was going to be something special. Unfortunately, he never produced the goods and carried his head high in the closing stages. He never seemed to enjoy jumping hurdles, although I must say he jumped much better on his last run. We have given him a long break and we know he has got ability so it may be just a matter of confidence. If we can find an easy race for him and he wins then it will do him the world of good. It may be that he is better on good ground.

SANTA CONCERTO (IRE) 10 ch g Orchestra - Sapristi
Is not getting any younger but he had a great season last year winning three races at Ayr. Unfortunately, the handicapper over reacted and he ended up giving lumps of weight to the likes of Step On Eyre and Young Kenny, who never stopped winning. He jumped well round Aintree and the Grand National is certainly a possibility. On the other hand, he loves Ayr and, if he has had a light campaign and the ground is not too firm, the Scottish National would be another possibility.

SPOOF (IRE) 4 b g Good Thyne (USA) - Wraparound Sue
A nice little horse who is not very big. He had shown speed at home prior to his bumper at Perth and I thought he ran well. We will try and win a bumper before going hurdling with him. Good ground should suit him.

SWANBISTER (IRE) 9 b g Roselier (FR) - Coolentallagh
Jumps and stays very well. He did well to win at Kelso after being beaten by the likes of Island Chief earlier in the season. At the time, he had appeared disappointing but looking back he had just come up against some useful rivals. He will be aimed at long distance handicap chases.

THE GREY DYER (IRE) 5 gr g Roselier (FR) - Tawny Kate (IRE)
A nice young horse who had a couple of runs last season. A typical Roselier, he looks like a tough staying type who will make a chaser eventually. He jumps well but he needs a bit more experience.

THE NEXT WALTZ (IRE) 8 b g Buckskin (FR) - Loge
Won the Channel Four Trophy for the most wins last season and I can't praise him enough. He always gives his best and ran a terrific race in the Scottish National. Obviously, he has gone up in the handicap both over hurdles and fences and he will be difficult to place. We will switch between the two and see what we can pick up.

TIME AFTER THYNE 6 b g Good Thyne (USA) - Lady Solstice
A big strong horse who picked up a bad knock last season so we stopped with him. He is OK now and he will remain over hurdles as he hasn't got the experience for fences yet. Chasing will be his long term game and he will begin the season off over two and a half miles.

TO-DAY TO-DAY (IRE) 6 b g Waajib - Balela
A strong horse and, providing he jumps well at home, we will give him a go over fences this season. Two and a half miles is his trip.

VALIGAN (IRE) 6 gr g Roselier (FR) - Wonderful Lilly
A tough horse by Roselier, he did well over hurdles last season. In many ways, he is similar to Birkdale and he jumps very well. The intention is to try and win another hurdle race and then we may send him chasing after Christmas. Three miles is his trip as he stays forever.

YANKEE JAMIE (IRE) 5 b g Strong Gale - Sparkling Opera
A well bred son of Strong Gale who has yet to run. He is bred for jumping and I would think he will go straight over hurdles. He is a big framed horse and he is likely to want some ease in the ground.

I have got a lovely set of unnamed young horses which have been broken and ought to be running in the second half of the season, in either bumpers or novice hurdles, and they should be worth looking out for.

4 b g Executive Perk - Sandy Jayne - bought at the 1998 Derby Sale, he is described as "a fabulous mover and looks a nice prospect."
4 b g Little Bighorn - Elegant Miss - also bought at the 1998 Derby Sale, he is owned by Ashleybank Investments.
5 b g Commanche Run - Deverell's Lady - bought at the 1998 Doncaster May Sales, he is described as "a lovely looking horse."
5yo gelding by Alphabatim from the family of Moondigua - "A lovely horse who's dam bred eight winners. He will run in my wife's colours."

FERDY MURPHY
Stables: Wynbury Stables, West Witton, North Yorkshire.
1998/99: 40 Winners from 221 Runners 18% Prize-Money £288,012
First-Time Out Winners: 11 20%
Hurdles & NH Flat: 23/132 17% Chases: 17/89 19%

TRACKS TO NOTE (Records from 1994/5 Season +):
PERTH 5/12 42%: MUSSELBURGH 11/35 31%: KELSO 6/20 30%: CARTMEL 3/12 25%.

TRAINER'S TIP FOR 1999/2000
BALLINCLAY KING (IRE) 5 b g Asir - Clonroche Artic
A very exciting horse who could go right to the very top. He has a serious engine. He won very well at Ayr and then went to Punchestown. Although he ran well the ground was horrible. There were good to firm patches and then bits of soft ground. He has done well over the Summer and he will follow a similar programme to what French Holly did as a novice. In all likelihood, he will start off at Ayr and then go to Haydock followed by a crack at the Tolworth Hurdle in the New Year at Sandown. Two miles is his trip and he is most definitely a Cheltenham horse.

ACKZO 6 b g Ardross - Trimar Gold
Will be going novice chasing this season and he really could be anything. He has got the potential to be top class. We purposely gave Cheltenham a miss last year as he needed to develop mentally as well as physically. He has really strengthened up and, while we may start him off over two and a half miles, he will get three later on.

ADDINGTON BOY (IRE) 11 br g Callernish - Ballaroe Bar
His whole season will be geared towards the Grand National again. He ran a smashing race last year and I think he would have finished even closer if the ground hadn't gone against him. He does love fast ground. The plan is to go to Aintree for the Becher Chase in November and then possibly back to Leopardstown after Christmas. In actual fact, there aren't that many races for a horse who is rated as high as he is.

ALBRIGHTON 4 b g Terimon - Bright-One
A nice little horse we bought out of Chris Thornton's yard. He won a couple of races last season and I can see him more than paying his way in two mile handicap hurdles this year. There is every chance that we may take him for a race in France later in the season. Likes good ground.

ALLETOTO   3 b g Mtoto - Allegory
We bought him at the Goffs France Mixed Sale at Saint-Cloud in July. He was a winner over a mile and a quarter and placed four times on the Flat in France. The plan is to send him three year old hurdling this season. He looks a nice horse.

ARDRINA   8 ch m Ardross - Ina's Farwell
Did well in staying novice chases last season winning three times in all. A very tough mare who likes a bit of cut in the ground. I will be disappointed if she can't win another handicap or two this season.

BECCA'S ROSE (IRE)   7 br m Lord Americo - Tarqogan's Rose
She is back in work and I expect to have her out in the early part of the Autumn. She likes good ground and three miles will be her trip. I am expecting her to pay her way.

BLUE MOON (IRE)   4 b g Scenic - Debach Delight
He was placed a couple of times in bumpers for Chris Thornton. We paid 20,000gns for him at the Doncaster May Sales and I am sure he will be worth following in two mile novice hurdles this season.

BREA HILL   6 b g Brotherly (USA) - Top Feather
He ran in bumpers last season but we are likely to bypass hurdling with him and send him straight over fences. Three miles will be his trip and he ought to win races.

BROOKSBY WHORLTON (IRE)   5 b g Commanche Run - Superlee (IRE)
Is owned by my Racing Club and he ran well on his only start last year in a Carlisle bumper, finishing fourth. Whether we give him another run in a bumper has yet to be decided but he is likely to want two and a half miles over hurdles.

CHRISTIANSTED (IRE)   4 ch g Soviet Lad (USA) - How True
Had a cracking season last year winning three times. He will continue to run on the Flat before being aimed at some decent handicap hurdles. There is a race at the Murphy's meeting at Cheltenham in November which we have got our eye on. Likes good ground.

COOLAW (IRE)   6 b g Miner's Lamp - Mijette
Missed the first half of last season but won both of his two starts later on. He is going novice chasing this year and Adrian (Maguire) is very excited about the prospect. While I am not totally convinced that he will be top class, I think he will make a very nice chaser and I can see him winning a big handicap one day. He will start off over two and a half miles.

COUNT KARMUSKI   7 b g Ardross - Trimar Gold
Won twice at Catterick last season and I am sure he will win more races this year. The biggest problem is that we are not sure what trip he wants. I think he wants two miles, his owner thinks two and a half and Adrian believes he needs three.

FRENCH HOLLY (USA)   8 b g Sir Ivor - Sans Dot
It is 90% certain that he will go for a race in France in November. After that, he will go novice chasing. We won't be aiming too high too soon and he will tell us if he is ready to take on the

top chasers come Gold Cup time. He jumps well at home and took to the French hurdles, which are mini fences anyway, extremely well during the Summer.

FRENCH WILLOW (IRE) 5 b m Un Desperado (FR) - Sit Elnaas (USA)
A nice filly who is owned by the same person as French Holly. She was unlucky to come up against a good horse of Jonjo O'Neill's at Hexham last season. Another who likes good ground, she definitely needs a trip. She will win her novice hurdles.

GENERAL LOUIS 5 b g Governor General - Model Lady
A gorgeous horse who has run well in bumpers. He is a real racehorse and will make a cracking novice hurdler this season. It is likely that he will begin over two and a half miles but I don't see why he shouldn't stay three.

GRANIT D'ESTRUVAL (FR) 5 b g Quart de Vin (FR) - Jalousie (FR)
Another very nice horse who ran well in a Haydock bumper. I wouldn't have thought he will have another run in a bumper as he really needs two and a half miles. He will win races.

KING'S CRUSADER (IRE) 6 b g King's Ride - Fern Glen
A lovely unraced horse who looks really nice. I hope to have him on the track by November and he will start off in a novice hurdle over two and a half miles. He could well be a Cheltenham horse.

MAC'S SUPREME (IRE) 7 b g Supreme Leader - Merry Breeze
Missed the whole of last season but we have had his legs done and I am looking forward to running him in two and a half mile novice hurdles. Before his injury he had won a bumper and run very well on his only start over hurdles. He will be suited by some cut in the ground.

NATIVE LEGEND (IRE) 4 b g Be My Native (USA) - Tickhill
A very, very nice horse who had a run in a bumper at the Punchestown Festival. His owner was keen to have a runner over there. He has plenty of toe and I would like to think we can win a bumper with him before going novice hurdling.

PADDY'S RETURN (IRE) 7 b g Kahyasi - Bayazida
Will go novice chasing and I plan to have him out reasonably early. I can see him running up a sequence of wins before the better novices run. The long term target would have to be the Royal & Sun Alliance Chase.

PARIS PIKE (IRE) 7 b g Satco (FR) - Bouise
A lovely horse we bought out of Paddy Mullins' yard. He made a winning start for us at Perth in May. He was bought for chasing and that is what he will be doing this season. I can see him making a very nice novice chaser in the North this season.

TONI'S TIP (IRE) 7 br g Phardante (FR) - Share The Dream
Another who won a couple last year and I can see him developing into a John Hughes type horse later in the season. He didn't run towards the end of last season because he had a slight touch of a leg but he is OK now.

Unnamed 4 b c Commanche Run - Knollwood Court
A very, very nice horse we bought at the Goffs Land Rover Sale in June. He is well related being a half brother to Sun Alliance Hurdle runner-up Judges Fancy and I can see him running in a bumper in the New Year.

Unnamed 4 b c Scenic - Sit Elnaas
We bought him at the Doncaster Spring Sales in May and he looks very nice indeed. We paid a fair bit for him and he is a half brother to French Willow.

Unnamed 4 b g Roselier (FR) - Ramble Bramble
He was bought as a three year old at the Derby Sales in Ireland. A full brother to Seven Towers, he is likely to be sent straight over hurdles this season. He looks a lovely horse and one to look forward to.

PAUL NICHOLLS
Stables: Heighes House, Manor Farm Stables, Ditcheat, Somerset.
1998/99: 110 Winners from 400 Runners 28% Prize-Money £1,192,565
First-Time Out Winners: 24 28%
Hurdles & NH Flat: 28/134 21% Chases: 82/266 31%

TRACKS TO NOTE (Records from 1994/5 Season +):
FONTWELL 27/63 43%: AYR 7/17 41%: SANDOWN 16/50 32%: WINCANTON 47/159 30%: CHEPSTOW 33/116 28%: WARWICK 10/37 27%: HEREFORD 11/43 26%: STRATFORD 9/37 24%.

TRAINER'S TIP FOR 1999/2000
YOUNG DEVEREAUX (IRE) 6 b or br g Lord Americo - Miss Iverk
Definitely a horse to look forward to. Having joined us from Ireland, he showed very little at home and we sent him to Chepstow for his first run and we thought he would finish sixth or seventh and, in the end, it was only greenness which beat him. He went back to Chepstow for his second run and he trotted up. Unfortunately he then picked up a minor leg injury which kept him off the track for the rest of the season. He is 100% now and will go novice chasing and he could be very interesting. Loves soft ground he will stay further than two miles.

ARLAS (FR) 4 b g Northern Fashion (USA) - Ribbon In Her Hair (USA)
A potentially very exciting horse who joined us from France during the Summer. He won a £50,000 Chase at Auteuil in May and the intention is to send him novice chasing after Christmas when he will get into all the good races with a healthy allowance. A very interesting prospect.

ASK THE NATIVES (IRE) 5 br g Be My Native (USA) - Ask The Lady
Will go straight novice hurdling over two and a half miles. Since joining us from Ireland he hadn't shown a great deal but he won his bumper in impressive fashion at Wincanton. You never know how good bumper form is but you couldn't fault his performance. Very much a future chaser, he would not want quick ground.

BENGERS MOOR 8 b g Town And Country - Quilpee Mai
Had one or two minor problems last year but he won well at Stratford in soft ground. He

probably should have won at Chepstow after that and you can forget his final run as he was over the top by then. I am sure he will win more races and he could be aimed at something like the Murphy's, if all goes well. Two and a half miles is probably his optimum but he will get three.

BETTER OFFER (IRE) 7 b g Waajib - Camden's Gift
We bought him out of Amanda Perrett's yard at the Doncaster Sales and the intention is to send him novice chasing. A likely starting point is at Chepstow on Mercedes Benz day, early in October.

BLUAGALE (IRE) 8 b g Strong Gale - Gentle Down (USA)
He picked up a slight leg injury after he won at Ludlow but he will be back after Christmas. I think he is a very decent horse and he could be an interesting proposition in a good handicap later in the season. Two and a half miles plus is his trip but he doesn't want soft ground.

BUCK'S PALACE 6 ch g Buckley - Lady Geneva
He is a real three mile chaser in the making and did very well to win a couple of novice hurdles last season. We have schooled him over fences and he jumps well. He will make a decent novice chaser, although he wouldn't want fast ground.

CALL EQUINAME 9 gr g Belfort (FR) - Cherry Season
More than did his job last season by winning the Queen Mother at Cheltenham. His season will again be geared towards the same race. In all likelihood, we will start him off in the Peterborough Chase and then, all being well, he will go for the King George. If he is going to stay three miles then he will do it round Kempton, especially on good ground. He is best fresh and he came back from Aintree last April with sore shins.

CALLING WILD (IRE) 9 b g Callernish - Chestnut Vale
Had an extremely good season winning over both hurdles and fences, including the Paddy Power Chase at Leopardstown. He jumped very well in Ireland. We then ran him too quickly at Haydock and he was still going well when he fell at Cheltenham. Loves soft ground and there is every chance that he will go back to Ireland at Christmas.

CHARLIE STRONG (IRE) 6 b g Strong Gale - The Village Vixen
Won a couple of point to points for Richard Barber last season. He looks a nice horse and the plan is to send him novice chasing.

DERRYMORE MIST (IRE) 7 ch g Le Bavard (FR) - Cheribond
I like him a lot. He won two races last season but suffered with sore shins. I thought he ran a cracking race at Cheltenham as he didn't come down the hill. He wouldn't want soft ground.

DINES (IRE) 7 b g Phardante (FR) - Dippers Daughter
A very tough horse who took extremely well to fences winning four races. By the end of last season he had just gone over the top. He is high in handicap now but he will win again. Better going right handed with two miles being his trip.

DOUBLE THRILLER 9 b g Dubassoff (USA) - Cape Thriller
Picked up a minor injury when running loose in the Grand National but he is OK now and he

will be coming back into work in September. We may well decide to follow a similar programme to last season by starting him off in the Jim Ford then the Gold Cup followed by the National again. The trip in the Gold Cup is not a problem. We will probably ride him differently next time by holding him up. I have no doubts that he has the ability to make up into a leading contender again, especially if you consider the improvement he showed last season compared to his point to point form.

EARTHMOVER (IRE) 8 ch g Mister Lord (USA) - Clare's Crystal
Was very disappointing last season. After he fell at Newton Abbot and came back badly injured we should have roughed him off for the season. He nearly died the following evening. His owners were keen to get him ready for Cheltenham and we were always rushing him. He is in work now and if we can get him back to his best then he is very well handicapped. We will probably start him off in the Mercedes Benz at Chepstow.

EMBATTLE 3 ch g Rock City - Sleepline Princess
He is a full brother to Rockforce and he has joined us from Mick Channon. Juvenile hurdling is the plan and he looks a nice horse.

EXISTENTIAL (FR) 4 b g Exit To Nowhere (USA) - Lyceana
He won a handicap on the Flat in Ireland in April and we bought him at the Doncaster Spring Sales. We haven't done anything with him yet but he looks a nice horse and he will hopefully make a decent novice hurdler.

EXTRA STOUT (IRE) 7 ch g Buckskin (FR) - Bold Strike (FR)
He has been bought to replace Belmont King who was getting too high in the handicap for his owner Mrs Bond. The plan is to aim him at three to four mile handicap chases and he is also still eligible for the National Chase at Cheltenham.

EXECUTIVE DECISION (IRE) 5 ch g Classic Music (USA) - Bengala (FR)
A very nice horse who had a minor breathing problem last season. It may have looked as though he wasn't going through with his challenges but the reason was because he was having trouble breathing. We are going to send him novice chasing and he loves soft ground.

FADALKO (FR) 6 b g Cadoudal (FR) - Kalliste (FR)
A very exciting prospect for novice chasing this season. He has schooled nicely and I am hoping he will turn out to be my Arkle horse. When he first arrived from France in the Autumn, he took a while to acclimatise. We kept trying him over further than two miles and it looked as though he wouldn't get the trip. However, now that he has settled in I wouldn't be against trying him over further again. He showed some excellent form in the Spring winning the Scottish Champion Hurdle. You can forget his last run at Haydock as he was over the top.

FATHER KRISMAS 4 ch g Kris - My Sister Ellen
While I think there are only two four year old novice chases before Christmas that is the plan as he will get allowances in the New Year. Two to two and a half miles on soft ground would be his ideal conditions.

FLAGSHIP THERESE (IRE) 5 br m Accordion - Maryland Flagship

A great mare who enjoyed a cracking season. The plan is to alternate between handicap hurdles and novice chases with her this year. The long term plan is the Gold Card Final at Cheltenham in March. She is not very big but she is a great jumper.

FLAGSHIP UBERALLES (IRE) 5 br g Accordion - Fourth Degree

A absolute star who kept on improving. He made remarkable progress for a five year old. The only time he got beaten over fences was over two and a half miles at Chepstow. He ran as though he didn't get the trip but I think the ground was a more important factor. It was far too soft and I shouldn't have run him. On good ground, I think he will stay. If he keeps on improving he could well be Call Equiname's chief danger. The Haldon Gold Cup at Exeter is his likely starting point.

FORTVILLE (FR) 5 ch g Mansonnien (FR) - Grand Yepa (FR)

He is a nice horse who was trained by Richard Barber last season. He was a little unlucky for Richard as he failed to complete on his first three starts in point to points but he won his maiden very easily in May. I think he will start off in novice hurdles this season.

GEDEON (FR) 5 b g Video Rock - Unite II

He is a lovely horse whom we bought in France during the Summer. He won a two and a half mile chase at Auteuil in May. The plan is go novice chasing with him and he looks a very interesting prospect.

GREEN GREEN DESERT (FR) 8 b g Green Desert (USA) - Green Leaf (USA)

We have been very pleased with him. He was only beaten eight lengths in the Queen Mother and he is now rated 156. Following Cheltenham, he trotted up at Ayr. As far as I am concerned, he is totally genuine and I may give him a try over two and a half miles.

HIGH GALE (IRE) 7 b g Strong Gale - High Board

Was lame at the end of last season. He had a tiny fracture and has spent two months in his box. Two mile handicap chases on fast ground suit him ideally.

IRBEE 7 b g Gunner B - Cupids Bower

Ran very consistently last year winning four times. He is best fresh and loves soft ground. I am sure he will win more races over two and a half miles and ought to be capable of winning a decent handicap.

JACK THE BEAR (IRE) 5 b g Un Desperado - Vale of Peace

A lovely big horse we bought at Doncaster in May. He won his only point to point in Ireland and the plan is to send him novice chasing. However, we won't be giving him a hard season as he is only a five year old.

JULIE'S LEADER (IRE) 5 b g Supreme Leader - Parkavoureen

He is a very, very nice horse who had one run in a bumper at Newton Abbot. We thought he would run very well as he had pleased us with his homework. However, he didn't quite live up to our expectations but we did find that he was suffering from sore shins.

JUYUSH (USA) 7 b g Silver Hawk (USA) - Silken Doll (USA)
He is obviously a horse with a lot of ability and we bought him at the Doncaster May Sales. The plan is to send him novice chasing straight away. We will take it slowly with him and see how he progresses before we starting making any big plans. Three miles will be his trip.

KNIGHT TEMPLAR (IRE) 6 b g Roselier (FR) - Rathsallagh Tartan
Did very well last year for a five year old and I can see him making up into a decent staying handicapper this season. He is bound to improve as he gets older.

LA MOLA SUN 5 b g Henbit (USA) - Moheli
A nice unraced horse who will more than likely start off in a bumper in the Autumn. He hasn't done an awful lot but what he has done has pleased us.

LAREDO (IRE) 6 b g Accordion - Amelita
Won three novice chases last season and I think he was unlucky not to win at Ascot when he fell at the last. Joe (Tizzard) thought he would have won. Two and a half mile handicaps are his future and I think he is more than capable of winning races off his current mark.

MICHEL DE MOEURS (FR) 4 b g Northern Fashion (USA) - See That Girl
He is another horse we bought in France during the Summer. He had some very good form on the Flat winning on five occasions and being placed in Listed company. We will send him novice hurdling and he could be very exciting.

MURT'S MAN (IRE) 5 b g Be My Native (USA) - Autumn Queen
A lovely horse who won his only point to point in Ireland last April. He actually won on the same card as Jack The Bear and looks a promising type. He is owned by John Hales who, of course, had One Man. I would think he will start off in novice hurdles.

NORSKI LAD 4 b g Niniski (USA) - Lady Norcliffe (USA)
Did extremely well and was virtually unbeaten last season. His only defeat came when he ran a stinker at Cheltenham on the same day that a few of mine ran badly. We have gelded him and he has done very well over the Summer. He is a fine big horse and the plan is to aim him at the Stayers' Hurdle. As well as staying very well, he has got a lot of speed and would have the pace to win over two miles given soft ground.

OUR TOMMY 6 ch g Ardross - Ina's Farewell
He won one of his two point to points last season for Richard Barber. His victory came in soft ground and he looks as though he stays well. Goes novice chasing.

PERCOLATOR (IRE) 5 b g Executive Perk - Cherry Jubilee
Had one run in a bumper last season and I was very pleased with him. He is a big strong chasing type but he will spend this season running in novice hurdles.

PIPPIN'S FORD 4 b g Shahanndeh - Shakoura (FR)
He has joined us this Summer having come from Ireland. He won his only bumper last season at Gowran Park in March. We have yet to decide whether to run him in another bumper or go straight novice hurdling. He looks a nice horse.

ROCKFORCE 7 ch g Rock City - Sleepline Princess
Kept on improving last year winning three and it would have been four but for slipping at the last at Newton Abbot. He has not been the easiest horse to train and he will be back after Christmas to run in two mile handicaps.

SATSHOON (IRE) 6 b g Satco (FR) - Tudor Lady
Was trained last season by Richard Barber and he did nothing wrong in winning all three of his starts in point to points. The form is not easy to assess so we won't be getting carried away. He will go novice chasing.

SEE MORE BUSINESS (IRE) 9 b g Seymour Hicks (FR) - Miss Redlands
Is in great form at present. I am still not really sure why he did not show his true form in the first half of last season. Before the Pillar Chase he hadn't been showing his usual sparkle even though he looked alright and he ran poorly. We put the blinkers on for the Gold Cup and they made a huge difference. It is likely we will keep them on. There is a valuable new chase at Down Royal (6th November) and it is likely he will start off there. Then the plan would be to go back to Chepstow for the Rehearsal followed by another possibly crack at the King George. However, although he has won the race, I am not totally convinced Kempton suits him. He will probably go to Ireland in the New Year before another crack at the Gold Cup. Having thought he wanted soft ground, I believe he is now a much better horse on good ground.

SILENCE REIGNS 5 b g Saddler's Hall (IRE) - Rensaler (USA)
I like him alot. He did well on the Flat before we bought him and we gave him just the one run last season. We ran him in the Supreme Novices' Hurdle at Cheltenham and, despite having a rushed preparation, he ran well. Two mile novice hurdles are his target this year.

SOLDAT (USA) 6 b g Bering - Sans Prix (USA)
He has joined us having previously been trained by David Nicholson. Despite having had his problems he is still only six and I think he will make a very nice novice chaser this season. He fractured his cannon bone last season but he is OK now and I am excited about the prospects of him going over fences.

THE HOBBIT (IRE) 6 ch g Mister Lord (USA) - Sustentation
Another promising horse who was trained by Richard Barber last season. He won two points and I would imagine he will go straight over fences. One of his victories came in soft ground.

TORDUFF EXPRESS (IRE) 8 b g Kambalda - Marhabtain
Started the season extremely well winning at Plumpton and the big handicap at Ascot. However, he was not given the best of rides in the Welsh National and he suffered with a minor problem after his run at Sandown. He will again be aimed at the decent staying handicaps and the softer the ground the better for him.

TORN SILK 5 b g Top Ville - Cut Velvet (USA)
Won a novice chase last season when trained by Paul Webber. Two mile handicap chases are his target this year. All of his best form appears to have come on decent ground.

YORKSHIRE EDITION (IRE) 6 br g Strong Gale - Rent A Card
Has always worked like a very good horse at home and, while he won two races last season, we have yet to see the best of him. I am hoping he will show it now he is going novice chasing. He jumps well at home and ought to win races.

DAVID NICHOLSON
Stables: Jackdaws Castle, Temple Guiting, Cheltenham, Gloucs.
1998/99: 76 Winners from 439 Runners 17% Prize-Money £878,720
First-Time Out Winners: 11 11%
Hurdles & NH Flat: 49/280 18% Chases: 27/159 17%
TRACKS TO NOTE (Records from 1994/5 Season +):
TOWCESTER 30/87 35%: STRATFORD 20/60 33%: MARKET RASEN 9/28 32%:
WORCESTER 27/86 31%: HEREFORD 10/36 28%: ASCOT 22/99 22%: WARWICK 25/112 22%.

TRAINER'S TIP FOR 1999/2000
WINDROSS 7 b g Ardross - Dans Le Vent
Won two novice hurdles last season and he will go chasing this year. We have schooled him and he jumps very well. Two and a half miles is his trip and, like his half brother Air Shot, he loves soft ground.

At the time of going to press, a number of horses had yet to return to Jackdaws Castle and therefore no plans could be made by Mr Nicholson as he was unsure of their future. These included: **Escartefigue, King On The Run, Mighty Moss, Native Recruit.**

AIR SHOT 9 b g Gunner B - Dans Le Vent
Missed last season but he is back now and I am looking forward to training him again this year. Three mile handicap chases in soft ground are ideal for him.

ANZUM 8 b g Ardross - Muznah
Did tremendously well last season winning the Stayers' Hurdle and he will remain over hurdles, with Cheltenham being the long term plan again. I don't know where he will start off yet but we will be looking for some soft ground.

CALL IT A DAY (IRE) 9 b g Callernish - Arctic Bavard
He will also follow a similar programme to last season with the Grand National, again, being his main target. I was delighted with his run in the race last season.

CAPTAIN ROBIN (IRE) 5 b g Supreme Leader - Gentle Madam
A nice young horse who has yet to run. We didn't do a lot with him last year but what he did do pleased us. It is likely he will start off in a bumper and then go novice hurdling later in the season.

CASTLE OWEN (IRE) 7 b g Castle Keep - Lady Owenette (IRE)
I was very pleased with his progress last season and he will now go novice chasing. Two and a half miles is his trip and he appears to go in any ground. We have yet to school him.

CASTLE SWEEP (IRE) 8 b g Castle Keep - Fairy Shot
Won both his novice chases last season but he is still eligible for novices as they came after the 1st of May. His jumping was good and I would expect him to reappear in October. Likes good to soft ground.

GO BALLISTIC 10 br g Celtic Cone - National Clover
Is in very good form and his season will be geared towards another crack at the Cheltenham Gold Cup. He will run in all the big three mile handicap chases along the way. I would think it is highly unlikely that he will run in the Grand National.

GOOD TIME MELODY (IRE) 6 b g Good Thyne (USA) - Raashideah
Missed last season having had a slight touch of a leg but is 100% now and he will go straight novice hurdling. I would think he will want every yard of two and a half miles.

HURRICANE LAMP 8 b g Derrylin - Lampstone
Was very consistent last year winning at Sandown and finishing third in the Grand Annual Chase at Cheltenham. He will follow a similar programme again this season.

LA LANDIERE 4 b f Synefos (USA) - As You Are
She is an ex-French trained filly, who finished second and fourth over a mile and a half on the Flat over there. We may give her a run on the Flat before sending her novice hurdling. She looks a nice filly.

LORD HAWKE (IRE) 5 b g Mandalus - Shuil Comeragh
A lovely young horse who we have yet to run. We did a fair bit with him last season at home and he looks a nice horse. He will start off in a bumper and then go novice hurdling.

LORD SCROOP (IRE) 5 br g Supreme Leader - Henry Woman (IRE)
Had one run in a bumper at Wetherby last season and he delighted us. Unfortunately, he got loose at home and hurt himself shortly afterwards so he never ran again. He is fine now and may have another run in a bumper before going novice hurdling. I would think he will want two and a half miles over hurdles.

MIDNIGHT LEGEND 8 b h Night Shift (USA) - Myth
He will have his first race of the season in the Northern Ireland Champion Hurdle at Down Royal in early November. It is a £100,000 race and it looks an ideal first race for him. There is a possibility that he will go novice chasing later in the season, although he has yet to be schooled.

MILADY ANA (IRE) 4 b f Generous (IRE) - Allegedly Blue (USA)
She is a nice filly who ran well in bumpers last season. We have schooled her and she will go novice hurdling over two and a half miles.

MULLIGAN (IRE) 9 ch g Callernish - Anaglogs Pet
Ran a fantastic race at Aintree last April and he will follow a very similar campaign to last season. Two and a half miles is his best trip.

PERK ALERT (IRE) 5 b g Executive Perk - Clondo Blue (IRE)
He will hopefully make a nice novice hurdler, having won a bumper last season at Warwick. Appears to go on any ground and he is likely to want two and a half miles.

PICKET PIECE 8 br g Shareef Dancer (USA) - Jouvencelle
He is not very big but there is every chance that we may send him novice chasing. Had a good season last year winning three and ran a cracking race at Aintree. Stays well and likes good to soft ground.

RELKEEL 10 gr g Relkino - Secret Keel
Has been a smashing horse for us over the years and he will be back again this season. If everything goes to plan, he will have his first race in the Bula Hurdle again. Then, all being well, he will be aimed at all the top two mile hurdle races.

ROCABEE (IRE) 5 b g Phardante (FR) - Auling
Will start the season off in two and a half mile novice hurdles but there is a chance that we may send him novice chasing after Christmas. We have yet to school him over fences.

RUSSELL ROAD (IRE) 7 br g Phardante (FR) - Burren Gale (IRE)
A fine big horse, he will go novice chasing and I'm hoping he will be very good. He wants at least two and a half miles with good to soft probably being his ideal ground. We have schooled him over fences at home and he jumps great.

SHOTGUN WILLY (IRE) 5 ch g Be My Native (USA) - Minorettes Girl
Will go straight over hurdles and I think he will be a nice horse. He had two runs in bumpers and I was delighted with him. I would think he will want two and a half miles over hurdles.

SIMBER HILL (IRE) 5 ch g Phardante (FR) - Princess Wager
Won a bumper at Bangor last season and he will go over hurdles. We have been happy with his schooling and he is likely to want a trip.

SPENDID (IRE) 7 b g Tidaro (USA) - Spendapromise
Will start the season off in either handicap or intermediate chases. He did everything right last season, including when winning at Aintree. He still has a way to go but I wouldn't totally rule out the Cheltenham Gold Cup for him.

THE GOOD KNIGHT (IRE) 7 b or br g Good Thyne (USA) - Serene River
Has been hobdayed and he will be going over fences this season. We have yet to school him but he is a nice big horse and I don't envisage any problems. Two and a half miles is his trip.

TOTO TOSCATO (FR) 5 b g Lesotho (USA) - Tosca de Bellouet (FR)
He would be one of our big hopes of the season. He will go straight over fences over two miles and you would like to think the Arkle will be a definite possibility. Likes softish ground and, while we haven't schooled him yet, he has been in France.

ZAFARABAD (IRE) 5 gr g Shernazar - Zarafa
He is another who goes two mile novice chasing and, again, I would like to think he will be very

good. He is a big strong horse and fences won't be a problem for him. We schooled him at the end of last season and he jumped very well. Likes good to soft ground.

JONJO O'NEILL
Stables: Ivy House, Skelton Wood End, Penrith, Cumbria.
1998/99: 38 Winners from 231 Runners 16% Prize-Money £216,074
First-Time Out Winners: 10 15%
Hurdles & NH Flat: 25/144 17% Chases: 13/87 15%

TRACKS TO NOTE (Records from 1994/5 Season +):
KELSO 12/46 26%: UTTOXETER 11/46 24%: CARTMEL 4/18 22%.

TRAINER'S TIP FOR 1999/2000
CASH FLOW (IRE) 8 b g Mister Lord (USA) - Turn A Coin
Missed last season due to a leg injury but he will be back this season and I am hoping he will make a nice handicap chaser. He was a good novice two seasons ago and I think he would have beaten Paperising at Ayr when they both fell at the last. Three miles plus is his trip and I just think he could pick up a decent prize this year.

BUZZ 4 b g Anshan - Ryewater Dream
We bought him out of Chris Thornton's yard and he has yet to run for us. It is possible we will give him a run on the Flat before we send him novice hurdling. He was bought for jumping and we will start him off over two miles.

CAMBRIAN DAWN 5 b g Danehill (USA) - Welsh Daylight
Won a bumper at Hexham towards the end of last season and I was very pleased with his progress. He will go straight novice hurdling now and I would think he will want two and a half miles. Likes good ground.

CARBURY CROSS 5 b g Mandalus - Brickley Gazette
Started the season well but I was disappointed with him afterwards. We will probably begin over hurdles again but there is every chance that we may send him novice chasing after Christmas. I am hoping he will make a nice chaser. Two and a half or even three miles suits him well.

CHARTER RIDGE (IRE) 6 b g Glacial Storm (USA) - Pure Spec
Will go straight novice chasing. I thought he was going to be a real nice horse but he disappointed me to begin with before winning towards the end of the season. To be honest, he didn't beat much but with another year under his belt he could be a different horse over fences. He does like good ground with two and a half to three miles being his optimum trip.

COPE WITH REALITY (IRE) 6 b g Danehill (USA) - Reality
Ran in Irish point to points before joining us and he has had his fair share of problems. In all likelihood, he will remain over hurdles this season but he will make a chaser. Good ground suits him well.

FAIRY RIDGE (IRE) 4 ch c Indian Ridge - Fairy Folk (IRE)
Will run in handicap hurdles this season and we will try and pick up what we can. He will start off again over two miles but I wouldn't rule out the possibility of him staying further.

GO BOLDLY (IRE) 5 ch g Sadler's Wells (USA) - Diavolina (USA)
I must admit I was disappointed with his run at Wetherby. I know it was a good race but he arrived with a big reputation and I thought he would prove better than that. We will take it steady to begin with over hurdles and let him prove himself before we start aiming too high. Two miles looks like being his trip.

HOPEFUL LORD (IRE) 7 b g Lord Americo - Billie Gibb
Has suffered with leg trouble in the past but he seems OK now and he will follow a similar campaign to last year, running in staying handicap chases. I will be disappointed if he can't win again.

HUNT HILL (IRE) 4 b g High Estate - Royaltess
Looked a very good horse when winning easily at Chepstow over Christmas but he then disappointed. The ground was very soft at Chepstow and that appeared to suit him well. He is a bit of a character and we may just run him in blinkers this season. We will start him off over two miles, although I think he will get further.

JUST AN EXCUSE (IRE) 6 b g Project Manager - Over The Seas
A very big horse who loves bottomless ground. He will go novice chasing and I will be disappointed if he doesn't make a better chaser than he was hurdler. Three miles is his minimum and he will stay four, if necessary.

LEGAL RIGHT (USA) 6 b g Alleged (USA) - Rose Red (USA)
A very difficult horse to keep right. He did, however, win a couple and I'm sure there are more races to be won with him. Two and a half miles is his trip and he wouldn't want extremes of ground.

LORD OF THE WEST (IRE) 10 b g Mister Lord (USA) - Caroline's Girl
Got a touch of a leg after winning at Doncaster last season so we gave him the rest of the year off. All being well, he will be back this season and he will be contesting the long distance handicap chases again. Likes good ground.

MASTER TERN (USA) 4 ch g Generous (IRE) - Young Hostess (FR)
Ran well without winning last season. He ought to win a small novice hurdle over two miles this year. He is another who likes good ground.

NAUGHTY FUTURE 10 ch g Scallywag - Sea Rambler
Loves heavy ground but he is not getting any younger. There is a chance that he may be sent hunter chasing this season. However, if I had my way, I would continue to run him in staying handicaps.

NOUSAYRI (IRE) 4 b g Slip Anchor - Noufiyla
Won a bumper at Perth in heavy ground and I think he could just be alright. In all probability,

we will give him another run in a bumper before going novice hurdling. By Slip Anchor, he is always likely to want some cut in the ground.

RADIATION (IRE) 6 ch g Orchestra - Bernish Lass
Although I was pleased with his progress over fences last season, I did think he might turn out to be a little bit better. He just lacks that bit of class. Very much a stayer, he will be aimed at handicaps. He wouldn't want extremes of ground.

SCRAHAN CROSS (IRE) 6 b or br g Be My Native (USA) - Angolass
Has plenty of ability but he is a very frustrating horse. He jumps well but can be a funny ride. Sometimes he doesn't settle and won't finish his races and other times he does settle but still won't finish his races. Still a novice over fences, he ought to win races. It is very difficult to assess his best trip but I would say two and a half miles plus is ideal.

SLEEPY RIVER (IRE) 8 ch g Over The River (FR) - Shreelane
Won a couple of races for us last season and, although we may start him off over hurdles again, he will almost certainly go chasing sometime this year. Two and a half to three miles is his trip.

TOUGH TEST (IRE) 9 ch g Lancastrian - Take Beating
Jarred a suspensory last year and he has taken along time to get over it. Providing he recovers completely, he will again be aimed at long distance handicap chases. He is getting a bit long in the tooth but, when he is right, he could still win a good chase.

WHO DARES WINS 6 b g Kala Shikari - Sarah's Venture
Is still a novice over hurdles and he became very frustrating last season. If there was one horse in the yard last year who I thought could win two or three, it was him. He does like soft ground and three miles is his trip. I am sure he will jump fences one day.

MARK PITMAN
Stables: Weathercock House, Upper Lambourn, Berkshire.
1998/99: 25 Winners from 133 Runners 19% Prize-Money £134,035
First-Time Out Winners: 10   31%
Hurdles & NH Flat: 20/94 21% Chases: 5/39 13%

TRACKS TO NOTE (Records from 1994/5 Season +):
HUNTINGDON 7/18 39%: NEWBURY 2/7 29%: FONTWELL 3/12 25%: SANDOWN 3/13 23%.

ASHLEY PARK (IRE) 5 b h Sadler's Wells (USA) - Maiden Concert
A lovely horse we bought out of Charles O'Brien's yard. He was a Group winner on the Flat and has always been very impressive at home. We took him to Sandown, for his hurdling debut, hoping he would win and he did so in some style. He jumped superbly and won very easily. Unfortunately he picked up a slight knock and had to miss the rest of the season. The plan is for him to come back at the end of November or beginning of December and he will, hopefully, have one run before Cheltenham. I would like to think he will prove good enough to run in the Champion Hurdle. He is a very classy horse who likes good ground.

CANASTA (IRE) 5 b g Buckskin (FR) - Bells Walk Fancy
Enjoyed a terrific year last season with his best run coming in the Festival bumper at Cheltenham when he finished third. I think he was unlucky not to finish even closer as he got blocked when he was starting his run and he lost his momentum. Jumps very well and he will go straight novice hurdling over two and a half miles. He looks the sort of horse who will stay well and will have no trouble getting three miles. Whether he will go to Cheltenham I don't know yet as I am not keen on running National Hunt bred horses against the Flat bred ones.

CARDINAL SINN (IRE) 4 b g Mister Lord (USA) - Polly-Glide
A very nice unraced horse who worked well last season. We were going to run him in a bumper at Newbury but the ground got too firm. He has been schooled over hurdles and he jumps very well. However, he will start off in a bumper and there is every chance that he may stick to bumpers this season and be aimed at the Festival bumper at Cheltenham. He would want good ground or softer.

CHERRYMORE (IRE) 8 br g Cataldi - Cherry Bow
Did not do a lot last season owing to one or two training problems but if he can be kept sound then I am sure he will make a useful chaser this year. He is OK now and he will go novice chasing over two and a half miles. He is a horse who has always promised a lot.

CIMARRONE COVE (IRE) 4 b g Roselier (FR) - Sugarstown
A very big horse who had one run in a bumper last season finishing a promising second at Towcester. He will obviously be going novice hurdling this season and he looks as though he is very much a stayer.

CONNOR MACLEOD (IRE) 6 ch g Torus - Blackrath Gem
Won a decent race at Cheltenham towards the end of last season. His future is really in the hands of the handicapper. If he is not too badly treated then he is likely to start the season off over hurdles and we will see how far we can go with him before going over fences. Very much a chaser in the making, we have yet to school him over fences. He would not want the ground too soft.

COUNT CAMPIONI (IRE) 5 br g Brush Aside (USA) - Emerald Flair
He is in a similar boat to 'Connor' in that we will see how far we can progress over hurdles before going chasing. A promising horse, I feel he ought to win again over hurdles. I think he wants a trip and we will probably step him up to three miles this year. Likes good ground.

EVER BLESSED (IRE) 7 b g Lafontaine (USA) - Sanctify
A very interesting horse for this season. He showed good form last season and was in the process of running a big race at Aintree when he fell. I feel he would have won that day as he had all his rivals on the rack. The plan is to aim him at the Hennessy and we will probably give him two runs beforehand.

GOODTIME GEORGE (IRE) 6 b g Strong Gale - Game Sunset
He is a full brother to Nicky Henderson's Stormyfairweather. He had a great year last season and will go novice chasing this time. A super jumper, he does not like the ground too soft. Obviously, the long term aim for him is the Royal & Sun Alliance Chase at Cheltenham.

HITMAN (IRE) 4 b g Contract Law (USA) - Loveville (USA)
Was a very high class horse on the Flat when trained by Henry Cecil. Unfortunately he got injured but he is OK now and he will go novice hurdling. We will take our time with him but potentially he is a very exciting prospect. A big horse with plenty of scope, he has a lot of class. Two miles will be his trip.

JET CLASSIFILES (IRE) 5 br g Good Thyne (USA) - Gamonda
Ran well on his only start last season in a Doncaster bumper finishing third. It is likely that he will go straight novice hurdling and I would imagine that he will stay very well.

JET TABS (IRE) 7 b g Roselier (FR) - Bell Walks Fancy
Another very interesting horse for this season. He is back in work now and I am hoping he will enjoy a successful year. Although his future lies over fences he will certainly start off this season over hurdles and I would like to think he can achieve a much higher rating than he is currently on.

JOHN DAVID 6 b g Broadsword (USA) - Celtic Well
A half brother to Teeton Mill, he was very impressive in winning his only bumper at Chepstow last season. Unfortunately, he got kicked on his hind leg as the tapes went up and, once he had recovered from that, he was being prepared for the Cheltenham bumper but then got a slight fracture in his knee. He is OK now but he is unlikely to be out before Christmas. Jumps very well, he will go novice hurdling before going chasing the following season.

KING OF THE CASTLE (IRE) 4 b g Cataldi - Monashuna
Looked a very impressive bumper horse last season winning both his starts. The plan is for him now to go straight over hurdles. While we hope he will go a long way over hurdles, we will start off low key and see how we go. He is very much a speed horse and two miles suits him well.

LORD OPTIMIST 6 br g Arctic Lord - Sweet Optimist
Ran well in his bumper at Fontwell staying on well to be fifth. In all likelihood, we will give him another run in a bumper before going novice hurdling. Once hurdling, he will want a trip.

MONSIGNOR (IRE) 5 ch g Mister Lord (USA) - Dooney's Daughter
Had a magnificent year which was crowned with his victory at the Cheltenham Festival. It was a tremendously gutsy effort. He goes hurdling now and I expect him to stay well. We will start him off over two and a half miles but long term he is very much a three miler. We have high hopes for him.

NERVOUS O'TOOLE (IRE) 4 b g Mister Lord (USA) - Dooney's Daughter
A full brother to Monsignor, he was very impressive when winning his bumper at Worcester. We are currently undecided what to do with him. May go novice hurdling or he may be kept to bumpers this season and aim him at the Festival bumper at Cheltenham. Whatever we decide, he is a very talented horse and he won't be over-raced this season.

PRESSURISE 4 ch g Sanglamore - Employ Force
He is a nice big horse we bought at the Ascot Sales in July. Previously trained by Sir Mark Prescott, he won three times on the Flat. He will be going novice hurdling this season but he will jump a fence in time.

QUEEN'S HARBOUR (IRE) 5 b g Brush Aside (USA) - Queenie Kelly
A great big horse who ran well in bumpers last season, winning a couple. Goes novice hurdling and looks a stayer. We will start off low key with him and let him win his races before tackling anything big. It wouldn't be a disaster if he missed Cheltenham this season and went for something like the EBF Final instead. A lovely horse.

SANTABLESS (IRE) 6 b g Zaffaran (USA) - Nimbi
Enjoyed a terrific season winning three races. He also ran a blinder at Aintree and then at Haydock in May. We have schooled him over fences and he jumps well and I think he could prove good enough to go to Cheltenham next March.

SCARLET EMPEROR (IRE) 5 b g Supreme Leader - Red Donna
Had a good season winning a couple of bumpers and has, also, won a novice hurdle. However, that win came after the 1st of May, so he is still qualified for novices this year. Likes good ground and he should more than pay his way.

SON OF LIGHT (IRE) 4 br g Hollow Hand - Leaney Kamscort
We were pleased with his run in a Worcester bumper, where he finished fourth. He was still quite weak last year but he has done well over the Summer. Will go novice hurdling this season, although he wouldn't want the ground too soft.

YEOMAN SAILOR (IRE) 5 b g Roselier (FR) - Liffey Lady
Made good progress last year winning at Wincanton and Fontwell. He is very much a chaser in the making but he will start this season off over hurdles, in handicaps. We will see how far he can go over hurdles before sending him chasing. Three miles will be his trip.

MARY REVELEY
Stables: Groundhill Farm, Lingdale, Saltburn, Cleveland.
1998/99: 104 Winners from 477 Runners 22% Prize-Money £515,016
First-Time Out Winners: 15   15%
Hurdles & NH Flat: 68/330 21% Chases: 36/147 24%

TRACKS TO NOTE (Records from 1994/5 Season +):

CARTMEL 5/13 38%: TOWCESTER 3/8 38%: HUNTINGDON 16/47 34%: CARLISLE 37/120 31%: PERTH 21/72 29%: KELSO 38/140 27%: MARKET RASEN 30/121 25%: NEWCASTLE 53/209 25%: CATTERICK 29/131 22%: SEDGEFIELD 48/216 22%: WETHERBY 43/204 21%.
TRAINER'S TIP FOR 1999/2000
"The novice chasers, in particular, should be worth following."

ALLOTROPE (IRE) 4 b g Nashwan (USA) - Graphite (USA)
We bought him at the Newmarket Sales last Autumn and the plan is for him to go novice hurdling. He has schooled OK at home and he will probably start off over two and a half miles. He may well run on the Flat again beforehand.

BROTHER OF IRIS (IRE) 6 b g Decent Fellow - Granita Cafe (FR)
Has made a full recovery from the accident he suffered in the Sun Alliance Chase at Cheltenham. All being well he will be back on the racecourse in November / December time and will be aimed at three mile handicap chases. He does like good ground and I would like to think he is reasonably well handicapped.

FOUNDRY LANE 8 b g Mtoto - Eider
Will go back over fences. His jumping appears to be getting better and, while I wouldn't say he is well handicapped, he ought to win more races. Two to two and a half miles is ideal and he appears to go on any ground.

FULLOPEP 5 b g Dunbeath (USA) - Suggia
Goes straight novice chasing and I think he will do well. He has schooled nicely at home with two to two and a half miles being his trip. He is from the family of Simply Dashing so you would expect him to make a nice chaser.

GRAY GRANITE (IRE) 4 b g Rock Hopper - Mrs Gray
A nice horse who won his bumper last season at Huntingdon. He is owned by my Racing Club. It's likely that he will have another run in a bumper and then go novice hurdling later in the season. He has always worked like a nice horse at home.

HALLYARDS GAEL (IRE) 5 br g Strong Gale - Secret Ocean
A very nice young horse who has yet to run. We will more than likely start him off in a bumper and then go novice hurdling. However, anything he does this season is a bonus as he is very much a chaser in the making.

HARFDECENT 8 b g Primitive Rising (USA) - Grand Queen
Has had his problems in the past and he never really got his ground last season. I'm sure he will win more races, though. Fast ground over two and a half miles would just about be his ideal conditions.

IL CAVALIERE 4 b g Mtoto - Kalmia
Another very nice horse who has won his only start, a bumper at Market Rasen in June. We like him a lot and there is every chance that he may stick to bumpers this season.

JOWOODY 6 ch m Gunner B - Maskwood
She has not yet come back in but there is a possibility that she will go novice chasing. She does like soft ground.

JUNE'S RIVER (IRE) 6 ch g Over The River (FR) - June Bug
Showed progressive form last season winning twice at Carlisle. He is another who likes soft ground and he will run in two mile handicap chases.

KATHRYN'S PET 6 b m Blakeney - Starky's Pet
Like Jowoody, we hope to send her novice chasing. She could be aimed at the two mile mares' only events.

KILCREGGAN 5 b g Landyap (USA) - Lehmans Lot
Ran in three bumpers last season and is currently running on the Flat. It is likely he will go novice hurdling over two miles towards the end of the year.

LINGDALE LAD (IRE) 5 b g Remainder Man - Pampered Sally
Ran very well when finishing second in an Ayr bumper. He is another potential chaser but will run in two and a half mile novice hurdles this season.

LLOYDEY BOY (IRE) 4 gr g Roselier (FR) - Bright Boreen
Another nicely bred unraced horse. The Roselier's tend to need plenty of time and that is what he will be given. He is undoubtedly a chaser in the making so he is likely to go straight over hurdles without a run in a bumper. A nice horse.

LORD LAMB 7 gr g Dunbeath (USA) - Caroline Lamb
Will have another run or two on the Flat before he goes back over hurdles. He will be aimed at some of the decent two mile handicaps. Good ground suits him best.

MARELLO 8 br m Supreme Leader - Clonmello
It has yet to be confirmed but I think the plan is to go novice chasing with her. She has been schooled over fences and she jumps very well. You would like to think she will develop into a good three mile novice chaser.

MERRY MASQUERADE (IRE) 8 b g King's Ride - Merry Madness
He will also be going novice chasing. A very big horse, he did well to win two handicap hurdles last season as he is definitely a chaser. He did have a slight setback halfway through last season but it was nothing serious. The softer the better for him with three miles his minimum.

MR BUSBY 6 b g La Grange Music - Top-Anna (IRE)
Won a couple of races last season and will go chasing this year. A big horse, he does like soft ground with two and a half miles being his trip.

OATH OF ALLEGIANCE (IRE) 4 b f Supreme Leader - Kasam
A lovely mare who has yet to see a racecourse. She will begin in a bumper and then go novice hurdling later in the season. I like her.

OCTOBER MIST (IRE) 5 gr g Roselier (FR) - Bonny Joe
A very nice horse who just had the one run last year. He finished second in a Wetherby bumper but he was still a little bit weak so we gave him time to develop. We have always liked him and he is a horse who has plenty of speed being from the family of Lord Dorcet. He is not really a typical Roselier in that respect. We will give him another run in a bumper before going novice hurdling.

RANDOM HARVEST (IRE) 10 br g Strong Gale - Bavello
Has done extremely well for us and he will continue to run in all the decent staying handicap chases over three miles. However, I don't think he would ever be suited by a race like the Grand National.

THE GRANBY (IRE) 5 b g Insan (USA) - Elteetee
A nice horse who likes fastish ground. He was unlucky last time at Market Rasen and I'm sure there are races to be won with him over two and a half miles.

TIME OF FLIGHT (IRE) 6 ch g Over The River (FR) - Icy Lou
A nice horse who is very much a chaser in the making and there is every chance that he may go straight over fences this season. He ran too badly to be true on his hurdles debut at Carlisle and I don't think it was the trip as I'm sure he will stay three miles alright.

TOM'S RIVER (IRE) 7 ch g Over The River (FR) - Nesford
Won a couple of novice chases last season and will be campaigned in handicaps over three miles at some of the lesser tracks.

TURNPOLE (IRE) 8 br g Satco (FR) - Mountain Chase
Will go chasing again this season. A lot depends on the handicapper. I just hope he handicaps him on his chasing form and not his hurdles form. Three miles in soft ground would be his favoured conditions.

WOODFIELD GALE (IRE) 6 b g Strong Gale - Excitable Lady
He is another who will be going novice chasing. We have schooled him and he jumps well at home. He has improved as he has got older. Likes good ground with two and a half miles being his optimum trip for now.

WYNYARD KNIGHT 7 b g Silly Prices - The White Lion
Has been a grand horse for us, winning three novices chases last season. Two miles is his trip and his handicap mark means he will have to run in some of the decent handicap chases.

WHAT'S THE CRAIC IN IRELAND ?

ALEXANDER BANQUET (IRE) 6 b g Glacial Storm (USA) - Black Nancy
OWNER: Mrs N. O'CALLAGHAN
TRAINER: W.P.MULLINS   FORM FIGURES: 11 - 11117
Having won all four of his starts over hurdles, Alexander Banquet went to Cheltenham for the Royal & Sun Alliance Hurdle as a major contender. Unfortunately, he was never travelling at any stage and came home a very disappointing seventh, nineteen lengths behind Barton. However, it was later revealed that he had suffered a hairline fracture of a front leg cannon bone. Earlier in the season, he won the Grade 1 Royal Bond Hurdle at Fairyhouse (Yld/Sft) by a head from Cardinal Hill, in a thrilling tussle from the last. He was also a seven lengths winner from Native Upmanship at Leopardstown (Sft/Hvy) in February. His two other victories came at Fairyhouse again (Yld/Sft) and Punchestown (Heavy). Alexander Banquet is now likely to go novice chasing and, if taking to it, could run up a sequence. A step up to three miles would open up even more options.

CHAMPAGNE NATIVE (IRE) 5 b g Be My Native (USA) - The Race Fly
OWNER: BACK STREET Syndicate
TRAINER: T.J.TAAFFE   FORM FIGURES: 2 - 111
"He has some engine," remarked Jason Titley after Champagne Native scored on his hurdles debut at Cork (Yld/Sft) in May by a dozen lengths. Still eligible for novices this season, this Ir21,000gns purchase had earlier won bumpers at Naas (Yld/Sft) in March and Fairyhouse (Yld) a month later. He is very much a future chaser but he looks sure to win races over the smaller obstacles this term, especially over two and a half miles plus. "I think the world of this horse and he has a very bright future," believes Tom Taaffe.

LE COUDRAY (FR) 5 b g Phantom Breeze - Mos Lie (FR)
OWNER: Mr J.P.McManus
TRAINER: A.P.O'BRIEN   FORM FIGURES: 12P
Le Coudray arrived in Ireland with a huge reputation having won five hurdles races at Auteuil in France and earned the title of leading French four year old hurdler. He made his Irish debut at Naas (2½ m : Heavy) in January and destroyed the opposition, including the useful Limestone Lad. Sent straight to Cheltenham, he looked sure to win the Stayers' Hurdle jumping the final flight only to be collared close home by Anzum. Whether he did not quite get home remains open for discussion, with his jockey Charlie Swan believing the gelding idled in front. Le Coudray's final run of the season can be ignored as he was patently over the top at Punchestown when pulling up early in the home straight. It will be interesting to see whether his connections decide to go chasing this season as he certainly has the physique. Whatever is decided, he is sure to win races. "The way he jumps, I'd say fences will suit him. He is a serious horse," believes Aidan O'Brien.

MYHEARTISBROKEN (IRE) 5 b g Broken Hearted - Lady Mearlane
OWNER: Exors of the Late Mrs J.J.GORDON
TRAINER: D.WACHMAN   FORM FIGURES: 1
There can have been fewer more impressive bumper winners in Ireland last season than

Myheartisbroken's twenty lengths demolition at Limerick (Sft/Hvy) in March. Leading with just over quarter of a mile to travel, he bounded clear of his rivals to win very easily. His win at Limerick was, in fact, his second career outing as he had fallen when clear in a point to point at Killeagh (Heavy) in January when he was backed from 3/1 into 6/4. His trainer David Wachman said of his Ir1,500gns purchase: "He was only ever going to run twice, and he would have won his point by thirty lengths but for falling at the second last. He's a nice horse."

NATIVE UPMANSHIP (IRE) 6 ch g Be My Native (USA) - Hi' Upham
OWNER: Mrs J.MAGNIER
TRAINER: A.L.T.MOORE   FORM FIGURES: 31 - 4712221
"He is bred to be a chaser. He will go over fences next season and, if he doesn't take to chasing, he is good enough to go for staying hurdles," commented Arthur Moore after Native Upmanship had destroyed some high class rivals in the Grade 1 Stanley Cooker Champion Novices' Hurdle at Punchestown (Yld) by upwards of five and a half lengths. He had earlier been placed behind the likes of Alexander Banquet, Cardinal Hill and Greenstead as well as winning at Leopardstown (Soft) in December by twenty lengths. However, it was the step up to two and a half miles at Punchestown, for the first time, which brought about a tremendous amount of improvement. There seems no reason why Native Upmanship will not stay three miles and he looks a serious contender for the Royal & Sun Alliance Chase at Cheltenham.

RINCE RI (IRE) 6 ch g Orchestra - Mildred's Ball
OWNER: Mr F.M.MORIARTY
TRAINER: T.M.WALSH   FORM FIGURES: 1114 - 11121
Rince Ri looked a chaser with a huge future when beating Promalee by nine lengths in the two and a half miles Grade 1 Power Gold Cup at Fairyhouse (Gd/Yld) in April. Despite his victory, his trainer Ted Walsh stated afterwards: "He's still only a six year old and, basically, he's a big raw horse who needs more experience." Well, given more time and more experience, then he really could be challenging for major honours this season and even the Cheltenham Gold Cup could be a realistic target. Rince Ri has a superb record at Navan (4 wins from 6 races) and he made his chasing debut there in November (Sft/Hvy) and he produced an excellent performance to beat Native Estates by eight lengths. His other wins last term came at Naas (Hvy & Sft/Hvy) twice in January and February. It wouldn't be at all surprising if Rince Ri is sent over to contest a number of the major handicaps in England this season.

ROYAL SIGNATURE (IRE) 5 b g Royal Fountain - Lovely Snoopy (IRE)
OWNER: Mr SEAMUS ROSS
TRAINER: T.M.WALSH   FORM FIGURES: 7509 - 1112
"He keeps galloping, will stay further and chasing will be his game next season," reported Ted Walsh after Royal Signature had won his third start of last season at Leopardstown (Soft) in March. The five year old was previously trained by Paddy Mullins and he won a Leopardstown bumper (Hvy) in December for the Goresbridge handler. It was shortly after that success that the son of Royal Fountain was bought by Walsh. His other victory came at Punchestown (Hvy) in a maiden hurdle in February and he rounded off the season with a five and a half lengths second to Winter Garden in a Grade 3 event at Fairyhouse (Yld). Royal Signature is a novice chaser to follow this term over two to two and a half miles.

SAXOPHONE (IRE) 6 b g Supreme Leader - Kitty Cullen
OWNER: Mrs P.J.CONWAY
TRAINER: J.T.R.DREAPER FORM FIGURES: 0 - 1F21
Jim Dreaper did well with novice chaser Harcon during the 1994/5 season and he appears to have a similar type in the making for this term in Saxophone. Not the most fluent of jumpers of hurdles, he was very impressive in beating Paris Pike by four and a half lengths, under eleven stone eleven, at Fairyhouse (Hvy) over three miles in February. Earlier in the year, he had shown enough speed to win over two miles three at Naas (Hvy) from What's Up Boys. "He does look a real chasing type and will probably have more respect for fences. He seems to love testing ground," believes his trainer.

SIBERIAN GALE (IRE) 7 b g Strong Gale - Siberian Princess
OWNER: Mr G.MULLINS
TRAINER: P.MULLINS   FORM FIGURES: 1 - 214611 - 411 - 1
Siberian Gale looked a most progressive novice chaser last term, hacking up at Navan (Hvy) in October and Roscommon (Yld/Sft) in May. He has, in fact, already run this term winning again at Roscommon (Firm) in June by six lengths from Shaihar. A shoulder muscle problem meant the son of Strong Gale missed the majority of last Winter but that did not concern his connections as he is believed to be a better horse on good ground. Bearing that in mind, it may be that Siberian Gale is sent over to England for all the major two and a half mile handicaps. Still relatively lightly raced, he could improve even more once asked to tackle three miles. A potentially top class chaser who should be noted at Cheltenham in March.

SUNSET LODGE (IRE) 7 ch g Electric - Collopy's Cross
OWNER: Mr M.E.WALSH
TRAINER: C.BYRNES   FORM FIGURES: 13 - 1116
We may not have seen Sunset Lodge since November but he has the ability to make a very exciting two mile novice chaser this season. A fourteen lengths bumper winner at Limerick (Hvy) in October, he then won his first two starts over hurdles at Fairyhouse (Yld/Sft) and Cork (Soft) in November. Slightly disappointing in the Grade 1 Royal Bond Hurdle at Fairyhouse (Yld/Sft), in finishing sixth to Alexander Banquet, his trainer Charles Byrnes believes; "He will be an even better horse this season."

SYDNEYTWOTHOUSAND (NZ) 9 b g Sir Sydney (NZ) - Quite A Surprise (NZ)
OWNER: Mrs Michael Watt
TRAINER: N.MEADE   FORM FIGURES: 2 - 4628 - 1P1
"He could be a serious horse because we felt that he may just need today's run after being off for some time," stated Noel Meade after his giant nine year old had won the Grade 1 Tripleprint Novices' Chase at Punchestown (Yld) by three lengths from Society Brief. It was a remarkable performance as the ex-Henrietta Knight trained gelding had fractured a pelvis when pulling up at Leopardstown's Christmas meeting. He had previously won a Fairyhouse (Yld/Sft) novice by twelve lengths from Tarthooth in November. Sydneytwothousand displayed the pace to win over two miles at Punchestown but it was interesting to read Noel Meade's comments after his Fairyhouse victory: "He looks an out and out stayer." Sydneytwothousand is a chaser very much to follow.

TO YOUR HONOUR (IRE) 6 ch g Buckskin (FR) - Classical Influence
OWNER: Mr H.M.DUNNE
TRAINER: F.FLOOD   FORM FIGURES: 1153 - 11131S
A high class bumper horse two seasons ago, To Your Honour took very well to hurdling last term winning four of his six starts and it may have been considerably more had he not slipped on a bend at Naas in January, fracturing a rib. The injury meant Francis Flood's gelding has not run since. He registered comfortable victories at Listowel (Sft/Hvy), Navan (Hvy & Sft/Hvy) twice and Leopardstown (Sft/Hvy). Despite being much better suited by two and a half miles, To Your Honour ran extremely well when third to Alexander Banquet in the Royal Bond Hurdle at Fairyhouse over two miles. Very well suited by plenty of cut in the ground, To Your Honour has the stamp of a chaser and looks an exciting novice for this term.

WELL RIDDEN 5 b g Gildoran - Rydewells Daughter
OWNER: Mr G.B.F.CLARKE
TRAINER: A.L.T.MOORE   FORM FIGURES: 1
Regardless of how many more races he wins, Well Ridden will go down in history as the final winner at Greenpark, Limerick. He was a very easy thirteen lengths winner of a bumper (Soft) there in March, suppling his jockey Daniel Howard with his first ever winner. From the family of Noddy's Ryde, his dam is a full sister to the dam of Teeton Mill. There are few shrewder operators than Arthur Moore and he is sure to get the best out of this five year old. Owned by Leopardstown vice-chairman Frank Clarke, don't be surprised if Well Ridden is a frequent raider to the Dublin venue. He looks a high class novice hurdler in the making.

YOULNEVERWALKALONE (IRE) 5 b g Montelimar (USA) - In My Time
OWNER: Mr J.P.McMANUS
TRAINER: C.ROCHE   FORM FIGURES: 1
"He's raw, but he has a lot more speed than Galmoy at this stage, so let's hope he's as good," remarked Christy Roche after this half brother to Galmoy and Dance Beat had won his sole start last term, a Leopardstown (Hvy) bumper in December by an easy five lengths. On the strength of that win he was made the automatic favourite for the Festival bumper at Cheltenham. Unfortunately, a slight setback picked up shortly afterwards meant Youlneverwalkalone did not take up that particular engagement. Nevertheless, he looks an outstanding talent and should be followed in novice hurdles this season.

YOUNG BUCK (IRE) 5 b g Glacial Storm (USA) - Lady Buck
OWNER: SWAN LAKE Racing Syndicate
TRAINER: N.MEADE   FORM FIGURES: 12
Bought for Ir17,500gns at the Derby Sales, Young Buck looked potentially top class when routing the opposition in a Fairyhouse (Yld) bumper in October, beating Supreme Venture by ten lengths. As a result, he was sent for a 'winners of one' bumper at Leopardstown (Hvy) in January and was made 5/4 favourite. However, he was found to have a slight leg problem afterwards and that explains why he only finished third (placed second), three and a half lengths behind Frezenium. Noel Meade holds the gelding in the highest esteem and he will be very disappointed if he is not far short of the top level over hurdles this season.

1998/1999 CHAMPION IRISH NATIONAL HUNT TRAINER
NOEL MEADE
Stables: Tu Va Stables, Castletown, Navan, Co. Meath.
1998/99: 77 Winners from 433 Runners 18% Prize-Money £611,402
First-Time Out Winners: 15 14%
Hurdles & NH Flat: 59/328 18% Chases: 18/105 17%

ADVOCAT (GER) 9 b g Dancing Brave (USA) - Amethysta (GER)
He is still a novice over fences and that is the plan this season. We have had his wind operated on during the Summer and we are hoping that will prove to be a success. He is certainly capable of winning races.

BOLEY LAD (IRE) 5 b g Decent Fellow - Miyana (FR)
A nice horse who won a bumper at Navan last season. It is likely that he will go straight over hurdles now and I would imagine we will start him off over two and a half miles. He does like some ease in the ground.

COCKNEY LAD (IRE) 10 ch g Camden Town - Big Bugs Bomb
He is obviously not getting any younger but he has still got his fair share of ability. We were disappointed with his run at Punchestown last time but we found that he had got an infection. Two to two and a half mile chases will be the plan but whether he comes to England again remains to be seen because he has never shown his best when he has travelled.

COQ HARDI DIAMOND (IRE) 5 b g King's Ride - Snoqualmie
A very nice horse. He is a big horse and was given an uninspiring ride by Tony Martin in the Land Rover bumper at Fairyhouse. He has done very well over the Summer and will go novice hurdling. Two and a half miles will be his trip to begin with. He is a full brother to Malcolm Jefferson's King's Measure.

DEEANN NATIVE (IRE) 5 ch g Be My Native (USA) - Nordic Fling
He is a nice unraced horse. The plan is to start him off in a bumper and then I would imagine he will go novice hurdling later in the season.

FABLE (USA) 3 b g Hansel (USA) - Aragon (USA)
He has been a very decent horse on the Flat and is currently rated 99. The plan, however, is to send him juvenile hurdling. Providing he stays the trip then he should make a useful novice.

FROZEN GROOM (FR) 4 b g Bering - Danagroom (USA)
A nice horse we bought in France, where he won a Listed race on the Flat. He won very easily at Naas in February and I suppose you could say he was a little disappointing afterwards. However, he has done very well during the Summer and I can see him making a much better horse this season. He does like some cut in the ground and he possesses an awful lot of speed. I think he will be a force in all the good two mile handicap hurdles.

GREENSTEAD (USA) 6 b g Green Dancer (USA) - Evening Air (USA)
He is another nice horse who may well go novice chasing this season. We have yet to make a definite decision and we have yet to school him, although he is a big horse being 16.1hh and he

jumps hurdles well. He is a horse who would not want extremes of ground and, while he has been running over two miles, there is no reason why he shouldn't stay further. If he takes to fences he could be very good.

HILL SOCIETY (IRE) 7 br g Law Society (USA) - Sun Screen

Has had a wind operation during the Summer and we are hoping that will make a difference as it was definitely affecting him last season. Ideally, I would say two and a quarter miles is his trip and it is likely he will come over to England for some of those good two to two and a half mile races. Despite running poorly in last March's Champion Chase, he has run well twice at Cheltenham in the past.

JOHNNY BRUSHASIDE (IRE) 6 b g Brush Aside (USA) - Flash Parade

I think he is potentially a very good chaser on good ground. We thought he wanted fast ground but he disappointed at Roscommon but he is definitely better than that. Two to two and a quarter miles is his trip as we tried him over further last season and he just did not stay. Given his conditions, he will win more races.

MAKEAWAY 5 b g Be My Native (USA) - Cruiseaway

He is a nice horse we have just bought. He finished third in a bumper at Tralee in June, keeping on well. I would imagine we will give him another run in a bumper before going novice hurdling.

MISS EMER (IRE) 4 b f Be My Native (USA) - Living Rough

She is a nice mare who won a couple of races last season. Two mile handicaps are her future and she does like good ground.

NATIVE DARA (IRE) 6 b g Be My Native (USA) - Birchwood

He is a lovely horse who will stay over hurdles this year. Loves soft ground and I can see him making up into a Ladbroke Hurdle contender. He possesses plenty of speed with two miles being his trip.

NATIVE ESTATES (IRE) 7 b g Be My Native (USA) - Sesetta

I am looking forward to him. He won his novice chase at Leopardstown and then next time he injured himself under his knee. It was unfortunate as he now has to take on the big boys without a great deal of experience but he is a quality horse and I am sure he can win a decent race. Two to two and a half miles would be his trip.

NOMADIC 5 gr g Kenmare (FR) - Legend of Arabia

Our original plan was to send him novice chasing this season but that was before the Cardinal died who was going to be aimed at the top hurdle races. Now we are not quite so sure. He ran an excellent race in the Champion Hurdle and I think he would have been even closer had we ridden him for a place. Instead we rode him to win and he just got caught after the last by the placed horses. He has certainly got the physique for fences and, if he takes to them, then I have no doubts that he will develop into a very good novice chaser. Two miles is his trip but I do think two and a half, over fences, would be within his capabilities.

OA BALDIXE (FR) 5 gr g Linamix (FR) - Bal d'Oa (FR)

We gave a lot of money for him after he had won a Group 3 race on the Flat in France. He had just the one run for us last season at Leopardstown but he ran very flat and he was virtually pulled up. He ran at a time when a few of mine disappointed. We decided to cut him and let him have the rest of the season off. He is a great jumper and a very strong galloper and we are hoping to aim him at all the good two mile novice hurdles.

PILLAR ROCK (USA) 3 b c Alysheba (USA) - Butterscotch Sauce (USA)
He won on the Flat at Gowran Park in May and has run well all season. It is likely that he will be sent juvenile hurdling and I think he will make a nice jumper.

RIVER PILOT 5 b h Unfuwain (USA) - Cut Ahead
A lovely horse who is a bit like Greenstead in that we are not quite sure whether to stay hurdling or go novice chasing. He is a brilliant athlete and, if he takes to fences, then he could really go places. While he does not want real soft ground, he does like some cut and he would have no difficulty staying two and a half miles as he gets two miles well on the Flat.

ROSES OF PICARDY (IRE) 6 br m Roselier (FR) - Super Leg
She stays very well and you can forget her last run as she was definitely not right. The intention is for her to go three mile novice chasing and, while she is not a huge mare, she is big enough to jump fences.

SALLIE'S GIRL (IRE) 6 b m Un Desperado - Katerina
She was great last season and the plan is for her to go novice chasing as well. The ground could never be too soft for her and she stays exceptionally well. We have obviously got high hopes of her over fences.

SNOW DRAGON (IRE) 5 b g Sharp Victor (USA) - Roblanna
He is another who will probably be going over fences this season. I have been very pleased with his progress during the Summer as he is quite a slow maturing horse. Loves soft ground and I think a trip will help him.

SUN STRAND (IRE) 5 ch g Phardante (FR) - Gaelic Sport
A lovely big horse who is a born chaser. We may start him off this season in a hurdle race but he will be going chasing sooner rather than later and I think he will be decent. Appears to go on any ground and three miles is his trip.

SYDNEY TWOTHOUSAND (NZ) 9 br g Sir Sydney (NZ) - Quite A Surprise (NZ)
We are very excited about him and his season will be geared towards either the Queen Mother Champion Chase or the Gold Cup. I genuinely don't know which route we will take. When he first arrived I thought he was a stayer but he produced a remarkable performance to win the Grade 3 novice at Punchestown over two miles. Whatever, he will run in some good races along the way. He seems to go in any ground.

TARASHAAN 4 b g Darshaan - Tarasova (USA)
We bought him for quite a few quid at the Newmarket Autumn Sales last year and we were going to send him novice hurdling last season but he wrapped himself so we gave him plenty of time to recover. He is OK now and will go hurdling. He is a very athletic horse and he had some decent Flat form when trained by Sir Mark Prescott, finishing fifth in the Cesarewitch.

THREE KINGS 6 gr g Arzanni - Chancebeg
He is a nice horse but he had trouble with his wind and had to have an operation. His form is good and he will go novice hurdling this season. He is still quite an immature horse and he comes from a good chasing family. I am expecting him to stay well.

WOODENBRIDGE NATIF (IRE) 4 b g Be My Native (USA) - Wintry Shower
A very nice horse who I think is a certain bumper winner. He likes easy ground and, once he goes hurdling, I would expect him to stay very well.

YOUNG BUCK (IRE) 5 ch g Glacial Storm (USA) - Lady Buck
A lovely horse who really could be anything. He injured his knee in a winners' bumper so we gave him the rest of the season off as we think so much of him. He is from the family of Buck House and we are hoping he might prove top class over hurdles. Has plenty of speed and two miles will be his trip.

BEST OF THE REST

Listed in the following category are a number of **NOVICE CHASERS** who are not included in the Top 50 prospects but are likely to be too good to miss altogether.

ASHMAN (IRE) 6 b g Ashmolean (USA) - Rhein Maiden
"He is a lovely horse and he will go novice chasing this season." **Sue Smith**
Trip: 2½ miles +   **Going: Good / Soft**

CHEVALIER ERRANT (IRE) 6 b or br g Strong Gale - Luminous Run
"Brendan (Powell) schooled him over three fences at the end of last season and it was poetry in motion. He may have one more run over hurdles before going chasing." **James Adam**
Trip: 2 - 2½ miles   **Going: Good**
* James Adam is also very keen on stablemate **TIGERBURNINGBRIGHT** for novice hurdles during 1999/2000 - "We haven't totally ruled Cheltenham out for him this season."

CHURCHTOWN GLEN (IRE) 6 b or br g Be My Native (USA) - Hill Side Glen
"He ran in Irish points as a younger horse and is very much a chasing type." **Steve Brookshaw**
Trip: 2½ miles   **Going: Good / Soft**

DO YE KNOW WHA (IRE) 7 b or br g Ajraas (USA) - Norton Princess
"I think he is going to be a top three mile chaser in time." **Roger Curtis.**
Trip: 3 miles   **Going: Good**

DYNAMIC LORD (IRE) 5 b or br g Mister Lord (USA) - Hill Side Glen
"He is a tremendous jumper and I will be disappointed if he doesn't turn out to be very good over fences." **Tom Tate**
Trip: 2 - 2½ miles   **Going: Good/Soft**

IN QUESTION 5 b or br g Deploy - Questionable
"We are hoping he will make a top class novice chaser." *The Winning Line* (Trained by Venetia Williams)
Trip: 2 miles   **Going: Good**

JUNGLI (IRE) 6 b g Be My Native (USA) - Simple Mind
"He is a very nice horse and he will make a smashing novice chaser." **Paul Webber.**
Trip: 2 - 2½ miles   **Going: Good / Soft**

LORDBERNIEBOUFFANT (IRE) 6 b g Denel (FR) - Noon Hunting
"We are hoping he will make a very decent novice chaser." **Raymond Anderson Green (Trained by Josh Gifford)**

MASTER PILGRIM 7 b g Supreme Leader - Patterdon
"I hoping he will make a very nice novice chaser this season." **Venetia Williams**
Trip: 2½ miles   **Going: Soft**

MERRY PATH (IRE) 5 br g Alphabatim (USA) - Smokey Path (IRE)
"He was still weak last season and chasing was always going to be his game." **Oliver Sherwood**
Trip: 2½ miles +   **Going: Good**

STRONG SPRAY (IRE) 6 b or br g Strong Gale - Shannon Spray
"He is a half brother to Eirespray and we think he is a very nice horse. We are going to send him chasing this season." **Sue Smith**
Trip: 2½ miles +   **Going: Good / Soft**

TEAATRAL 5 b g Saddlers' Hall (IRE) - La Cabrilla
"He jumps well and will one day make a nice chaser." **Charlie Egerton**
Trip: 2½ miles   **Going: Good / Soft**
* He has raced Right Handed on 7 occasions, winning 6 times.

BUMPERS TO JUMPERS

The following horses all contested 'bumpers' last season and are more than expected to make their mark in novice hurdles this term.

DEALER'S CHOICE (IRE) 5 gr g Roselier (FR) - Cam Flower VII
Trainer: O.M.C.SHERWOOD   Career Form Figures: 1
Owner: Mr B.T.STEWART-BROWN
"He'll have a holiday and then go over hurdles but you won't see the best of him until fences," stated Oliver Sherwood after Dealer's Choice had made a winning debut in a Fontwell (Good) bumper in April. Despite running very green up the home straight, the son of Roselier took up the running with a quarter of a mile to run and stayed on powerfully to score decisively from Ray Source by two lengths. Oliver Sherwood has bought some terrific horses off Tom Costello in Ireland and Dealer's Choice looks like being the latest success story.

DORAN'S GOLD 5 b g Gildoran - Cindie Girl
Trainer: Miss H.C.KNIGHT   **Career Form Figures: 2**
Owner: Mr TREVOR HEMMINGS

"I think the world of this horse - I really think he could be quite special. He's only a baby and was bought as a three mile chaser," remarked Henrietta Knight after Doran's Gold had made a smashing start to his career when finishing second in a Sandown (Gd/Sft) bumper. Backed into 12/1 from 14/1, the son of Gildoran stayed on up the Sandown hill in tremendous fashion to claim second place, one and a quarter lengths behind Frosty Canyon. Bought for Ir34,000gns, the latest news from the Knight camp is that Doran's Gold will not be over-raced this season but he should more than make his mark in novice hurdles this term.

LANGHOLM VENTURE (IRE) 6 gr g Supreme Leader - Tara's Lady
Trainer: N.G.RICHARDS   **Career Form Figures: 2**
Owner: ASHLEYBANK INVESTMENTS Ltd.

Bought as a three year old for Ir12,000gns, Langholm Venture has been given plenty of time to develop and looked an excellent long term prospect when finishing second in a competitive Haydock (Soft) bumper. Very much a chaser in the making, he stayed on well to take second behind the easy winner Good Heart. Doing all his best work at the finish, Langholm Venture will be most effective over at least two and a half miles over hurdles. He will take some beating in northern staying novice hurdles.

LIGHTNING STRIKES (IRE) 5 b g Zaffaran (USA) - Nimbi
Trainer: O.M.C.SHERWOOD   **Career Form Figures: 231**
Owner: Mr R.B.HOLT

Lightning Strikes looked a horse to follow when winning a Uttoxeter bumper (Good) by five lengths in May. He appeared to appreciate the better ground having run well on much softer surfaces at Folkestone (Heavy) and Newbury (Soft) in January and March respectively. On the latter occasion he had got to within three lengths of the very useful Queen's Harbour and, on the former, he was beaten just a length by Itsonlyme. Oliver Sherwood has always thought a lot of this son of Zaffaran and he should develop into a very decent novice hurdler, especially over two and a half miles.

NO FORECAST (IRE) 5 b g Executive Perk - Guess Twice
Trainer: S.E.H.SHERWOOD   **Career Form Figures: 5120**
Owner: UPLANDS BLOODSTOCK

Simon Sherwood considers the ex-Irish pointer No Forecast to be the pick of his novice hurdlers for this term. His sole success from his four starts last season came at Folkestone (Soft) in December when he beat Au Lac by three lengths. However, he ran some tremendous races in defeat, notably when four lengths second to Golden Alpha at Newbury (Good) in February. Adrian Maguire, who rode No Forecast at the Berkshire track, reportedly thinks he could develop into a serious Royal & Sun Alliance Hurdle contender.

ONE NATION (IRE) 4 br g Be My Native (USA) - Diklers Run
Trainer: Miss H.C.KNIGHT   Career Form Figures: 3
Owner: The EARL CADOGAN
Prior to his debut at Ascot (Gd/Fm) in March, One Nation had been well touted in the racing press that he had been working like a class horse at home. When he did appear in a bumper, he was given an opening price of 7/4. One Nation did eventually drift out to 3/1 and, despite not winning, he did make a most satisfying start to his career in finishing third. Turning for home, the son of Be My Native was, literally, cantering but once let down, he showed distinct signs of greenness and was run out of it inside the final furlong. In the end, he was beaten four lengths and a head by Barney Knows. One Nation apparently delighted his trainer and he may well have another run in a bumper before going hurdling.

OSOSHOT 6 b g Teenoso (USA) - Duckdown
Trainer: Miss V.M.WILLIAMS   Career Form Figures: 1
Owner: Mrs J.HORTON
Despite being a six year old we have only seen Ososhot in public once. However, it was enough to tell us that he is potentially a very smart recruit to the hurdling ranks. Bought for 24,000gns as a four year old, he is a half brother to the 1988 Champion Hurdle winner Celtic Shot. Word had obviously reached Ludlow (Soft) that he had shown plenty of promise at home as he was sent off a 7/4 favourite for his racecourse debut in a bumper. Confidently ridden by Norman Williamson, he never looked in the slightest danger as he beat Derrintogher Yank by a hard held five lengths. The clock confirmed it was the performance of an exciting prospect.

ROSCO 5 b g Roscoe Blake - Silva Linda
Trainer: J.T.GIFFORD   Career Form Figures: 2
Owner: Miss J.SEMPLE & Mr J.T.GIFFORD
"He is a lovely horse who delighted us with his run at Sandown," commented Josh Gifford's son Nick, during the Summer regarding Rosco's very encouraging debut in a Sandown (Soft) bumper in March. This 40,000gns purchase looked to have plenty to do with a quarter of a mile to run but once the penny dropped and he knew what was required, Philip Hide's mount really stayed on with some effect to grab the runners-up berth, three and a half lengths behind Dusk Duel. Very much a chaser in the making, Rosco is held in some regard by the Findon camp.

SPECS (IRE) 5 b g Be My Native (USA) - Bambinella
Trainer: S.E.H.SHERWOOD   Career Form Figures: 01
Owner: UPLANDS BLOODSTOCK
Despite pulling up in his only point to point in Ireland in 1998, Specs arrived in Britain with quite a reputation. However, he displayed very little of his undoubted ability on his Rules debut in a Doncaster (Good) bumper in December, finishing only tenth of eighteen. Given time to acclimatise, he looked a totally different horse when he demolished eight rivals by upwards of seven lengths in a similar event at Newbury (Gd/Fm) in March. Graham Bradley asked the bare minimum from the son of Be My

Native and he lengthened in the manner of a very decent horse. He will have no problem staying at least two and a half miles over hurdles.

SPRING GROVE (IRE) 4 b g Mandalus - Lucy Lorraine (IRE)
Trainer: R.H.ALNER   Career Form Figures: 1
Owner: Mr H.V.PERRY

Robert Alner may not be renowed for his bumper horses but he introduced a lovely young horse in Spring Grove who scored in facile style at Chepstow (Gd/Sft) in March. Always cantering for Andrew Thornton, Spring Grove displayed an impressive turn of foot inside the final furlong and beat Philip Hobbs' Antique Gold by one and a half lengths. The winning margin could have been considerably larger had his jockey wished. It is to be hoped that Spring Grove will go some way to compensate the sad loss last season of Bramshaw Wood, who had looked such a promising chaser for the Alner yard.

THREE DAYS REIGN (IRE) 5 br g Camden Town - Little Treat
Trainer: S.E.H.SHERWOOD   Career Form Figures: 2

Another horse who contested a Chepstow (Good) bumper towards the end of last season and displayed an abundance of talent was the Simon Sherwood trained Three Days Reign. A son of Camden Town, he was not unduly punished on his debut by Dean Gallagher in the closing stages yet was only beaten half a length by Admiral Rose. It may not have appeared a particularly strong event but the third Route Two was a previous winner and the fifth home, Runner Bean, won at Uttoxeter subsequently. A reproduction of this run will see Three Days Reign in the winners' enclosure on a regular basis this season.

THE TOP 30 BUMPER RATINGS

By STEVE JOHNSON

NOTE: + + = Scope to improve considerably
+ = Likely to be capable of better

RATING	HORSE	TRAINER
97	Monsignor	Mark Pitman
96 +	Golden Alpha	Martin Pipe
93	Myheartisbroken	David Wachman
91	Our Bid	Kevin Prendergast
91	Queen's Harbour	Mark Pitman
90 +	Crocadee	Venetia Williams
90	Biliverdin	Sheena Collins
89	Frosty Canyon	Paul Webber
88	Billywill	Christy Roche
88	Canasta	Mark Pitman
88	No Forecast	Simon Sherwood
87	Alexander Prize	Willie Mullins
86 +	Ballinclay King	Ferdy Murphy
84	Baccarat	Jimmy FitzGerald
84	Ballet-K	Jim Neville
83	Knockalassa	Michael Cunningham
82 + +	Frenchman's Creek	Hughie Morrison
82	Aonfocaleile	Edward O'Grady
82	Bob What	Paddy Mullins
82	Minella Hotel	John Nallen
81	Errand Boy	Sue Smith
80 + +	Dainty Daisy	Francis Flood
80	Toggi Dancer	Nicky Richards
79	Matt Holland	Lucy Wadham
78 + +	King of the Castle	Mark Pitman
78 + +	Lord of the Sky	Lenny Lungo
78 +	Be My Royal	Willie Mullins
78 +	Betterthinkagain	Paddy Mullins
78 +	Itsonlyme	Venetia Williams
77 + +	John David	Mark Pitman

CHANGING CODES

Below are a selection of horses who have been running on the Flat this Summer but are expected to make a successful transition to the Jumping game this season.

ACQUIRE NOT DESIRE 3 ch c Woodman (USA) - Forladiesonly
Trainer: C.J.MANN.   Official Flat Rating: -
Previously trained by Criquette Head in France, where he won and was placed in Listed company. Bought for 18,500gns at the Newmarket July Sales.

BULLET 4 b g Alhijaz - Beacon
Trainer: D.M.TODHUNTER.   Official Flat Rating: 75
Bought privately out of Willie Haggas' yard to go novice hurdling, he is twice a winner on the level this Summer.

DARIALANN (IRE) 4 b g Kahyasi - Delsy
Trainer: D.K.WELD   Official Flat Rating: -
A half brother to 1984 French Derby winner Darshaan, he was trained last season by Alain de Royer-Dupre in France where he was placed. A winner of a Leopardstown maiden in July.

EVENING WORLD (FR) 4 ch c Bering - Pivoine (USA)
Trainer: M.C.PIPE.   Official Flat Rating: 107
Ran a tremendous race on his first start for Martin Pipe when beaten a short head in Class A event at Sandown in May. Likes soft ground.

FAR CRY (IRE) 4 b g Pharly (FR) - Darabaka (IRE)
Trainer: M.C.PIPE.   Official Flat Rating: 96
Bought out of Sir Mark Prescott's yard for 35,000gns at the Doncaster March Sales, he has already won the Queen's Prize and the Northumberland Plate for his new connections.

GENERAL CLONEY 3 ch g Simply Great (FR) - Kitty's Sister
Trainer: W.P.MULLINS.   Official Flat Rating: 93
Has shown tremendous improvement on the Flat this Summer winning four races on the trot, including the Listed Ulster Harp Derby at Down Royal in July.

GRINKOV (IRE) 4 b or br g Soviet Lad (USA) - Tallow Hill
Trainer: H.MORRISON.   **Official Flat Rating: 82**
"I think he will make a very good hurdler but there is a possibility that he will be sold at the end of the Flat season," remarked Hughie Morrison during the Summer. A very consistent handicapper, he won a competitive Newbury handicap in April.

HITMAN (IRE) 4 b g Contract Law (USA) - Loveville (USA)
Trainer: M.A.PITMAN.   **Official Flat Rating: -**
Very promising three year old when trained by Henry Cecil. Won Yarmouth maiden and Newmarket handicap. Placed in Group 3 Gordon Stakes.

INDUCEMENT 3 ch c Sabrehill - Verchinina
Trainer: Mrs A.J.PERRETT.   **Official Flat Rating: 88**
The winner of a £7,295 handicap at Sandown in June, he was bought out of Barry Hills' yard for 32,000gns at the Newmarket July Sales.

KEZ 3 b g Polar Falcon (USA) - Briggsmaid
Trainer: P.R.WEBBER   **Official Flat Rating: 80**
Trained during the Summer by Sean Woods, he finished second in a Newcastle maiden in July but will join Paul Webber to go hurdling.

KINGSTON VENTURE 3 b g Interrex (CAN) - Tricata
Trainer: W.G.M.TURNER.   **Official Flat Rating: 95**
"Bill (Turner) has always said this horse could end up at Cheltenham," reported Owner, Corinne Overton, after the three year old had landed his second victory of the 1999 Flat season at Lingfield in May.

LIGNE GAGNANTE (IRE) 3 b g Turtle Island (IRE) - Lightino
Trainer: MISS V.M.WILLIAMS.   **Official Flat Rating: 85**
Currently trained by William Haggas for *The Winning Line*, he has won all three of his starts this season. Racing Manager Hwyel Davies stated after his most recent victory at Newcastle in June: "There is a possibility he will go for some decent three year old hurdle races in the Autumn."

MIXSTERTHETRIXSTER (USA) 3 b g Alleged (USA) - Parliament House (USA)
Trainer: T.D.EASTERBY.   **Official Flat Rating: 98**
A very useful juvenile, he has failed to show his best form this term but he has been gelded during the Summer and he may go novice hurdling.

SARAYAN (IRE) 4 b c Lahib - Yaqatha
Trainer: D.C.O'BRIEN.   **Official Flat Rating: 87**
Bought out of Kevin Prendergast's stable for 32,000gns at the Newmarket July Sales. He was beaten a neck in a competitive handicap at The Curragh in June. "He looks a very nice horse and Cheltenham is the aim," reported Dan O'Brien about his new purchase.

SENANJAR (IRE) 4 b g Kahyasi - Sendana
Trainer: M.J.P.O'BRIEN.   **Official Flat Rating: -**
Bought for Ir33,000gns at the Goffs February Mixed Sale. Previously trained by Alain de Royer-Dupre for whom he won twice in France.

SIR ECHO (FR) 3 b c Saumarez - Echoes (FR)
Trainer: H.D.N.CANDY.   **Official Flat Rating: 85**
Selected in the hope that he may be sent to Martin Pipe. Owned by Peter Deal of Make A Stand fame, he won a maiden at Newbury in June and has the size and scope to make a high class novice hurdler.

SUPER WHIZZ 3 b g Belmez (USA) - Sliprail (USA)
Trainer: W.P.MULLINS.   **Official Flat Rating: -**
"We haven't backed him for the Triumph Hurdle yet. We'll be aiming him that way as he's built like a real hurdler," stated Willie Mullins after Super Whizz had won a Cork nine furlong maiden in April.

YEOMAN'S POINT (IRE) 3 b c Sadler's Wells (USA) - Truly Bound (USA)
Trainer: A.P.O'BRIEN.   **Official Flat Rating: 105**
"He's very tough and should make a lovely hurdler. This horse is something like Istabraq was at the same stage of his career. I'd imagine he'll go hurdling later in the year," remarked Aidan O'Brien after the potentially very exciting three year old had won the Listed Challenge Stakes at Leopardstown in July.

HUNTERS FOR PUNTERS

Selected below are horses which made a big impression on the point to point or hunter chase circuit last season and are expected to more than make their mark once again.

ACOUSTIC (IRE) 5 br g Orchestra - Rambling Ivy
Owner: Miss J.Taylor   **1999 Form Figures: 1**
Trainer: Andrew Dalton
Wetherby's (LH: Gd/Sft) point to point fixture in March saw the debut of the five year old Acoustic, and what a debut it proved to be. Cruising to the lead at the fifteenth, he was eight lengths clear by the second last, and came home hard on the bridle to beat Cherry Tart by eight lengths. You were very unlikely to see a more impressive winner all season and his progress this year must be monitored.

ALSTOE 5 b g Broadsword (USA) - Pollys Toi
Owner: Mr J.Nellis   **1999 Form Figures: 11**
Trainer: Tim Walford
One of the most exciting Northern pointers last season was undoubtedly the Tim Walford trained Alstoe. He won both his starts very emphatically. Displaying an excellent turn of foot on his debut in February at Wetherby PTP (LH: Good), he beat Elver Spring by two lengths. Alstoe then followed that success up with an equally easy four lengths victory at Stainton (RH: Soft) in April. The five year old still appeared green last season but with another Summer behind him we could really see something special from this fascinating son of Broadsword.

BOULTA (IRE) 5 ch g Commanche Run - Boulta View

Owner: Mrs C.Moore   **1999 Form Figures: 1**
Trainer: Clare Moore

Clare Moore has done very well with the useful Northern 'hunter' Coole Abbey over the past two seasons and she looks to have another interesting proposition for hunter chases in the once raced Boulta. He was a comfortable three lengths winner of an Open Maiden at Alnick (LH: Good) in February. Ridden by Mark Bradburne, Boulta took up the running at the second last and quickly asserted his authority to score readily. The form of his victory may not amount to a great deal but there was no faulting his performance.

CASTLE MANE (IRE) 7 ch g Carlingford Castle - Mantilla Run

Owner: Mr C.Dixey   **1999 Form Figures: 11111**
Trainer: Caroline Bailey

Castle Mane more than justified his place in last season's *One Jump Ahead* by winning all five of his starts, culminating in a thirteen lengths victory in the Foxhunters' Chase at the Cheltenham Festival. There were reputedly a number of offers made for Castle Mane subsequently but they were all turned down by his owner and the plan remains for him to start the new season off in hunter chases. Caroline Bailey believes, "he could be top class," and Castle Mane's early runs will tell his connections if he is good enough to go for the Foxhunters again or the Cheltenham Gold Cup. The seven year old has winning form on good and soft ground.

CURLY SPENCER (IRE) 5 br g Yashgan - Tim's Brief

Owner: Mr R.A.Bartlett   **1999 Form Figures: 1F1**
Trainer: Ronnie Bartlett

Curly Spencer looks a name to note for the new Millennium, judging by his three starts last season in point to points. An easy twenty lengths success on his debut at Lanark (RH: Heavy) in March was followed by an unlucky fall at Lockerbie (RH: Good), when travelling like a winner. However, it was his third and final run which really marked him down as a future 'hunter' to follow. It came at Balcormo Mains in April and he demolished his ten rivals by upwards of five lengths. Very confidently ridden by Andrew Parker, he was pushed out to beat Thosewerethedays, who had earlier won a maiden by thirteen lengths.

DONALLACH MOR (IRE) 7 b g Phardante (FR) - Panalee

Owner: Mrs C.Sample   **1999 Form Figures: 11**
Trainer: Venetia Williams

Everybody knows what Venetia Williams achieved with Teeton Mill last season having progressed through the pointing ranks and she must be looking forward to training a similar type in Donallach Mor. The plan is for him to run in novice chases this season and he looks one to follow, judging by his two wins last term. A comfortable eight lengths winner of a hunter chase at Huntingdon (RH: Good) in April was followed by an emphatic nine lengths success over Nethertara in the Weatherbys Champion Novices' Hunter Chase (for the John Corbet Cup) at Stratford (LH: Good) a month later. Very much one to follow.

MIGHTY STRONG 5 b g Strong Gale - Muffet's Spider
Owner: Mrs P.M.Shirley-Beaven 1999 Form Figures: 1
Trainer: Mrs P.M.Shirley-Beaven
Mighty Strong landed something of a gamble when winning on his racecourse debut at Tranwell (LH: Good) in April. Backed from an opening 6/1, he ended up a 4/6 favourite and justified his market support in some style. Well ridden by Pauline Robson, the son of Strong Gale displayed an explosive turn of foot to beat Baltic Lake by twenty lengths. The clock confirmed it was an excellent first effort as Mighty Strong won in a time of four seconds faster than the other division on the same card.

SUPREME LAD (IRE) 5 b g Supreme Leader - April Shade
Owner: Mrs A.M.Easterby   1999 Form Figures: 1
Trainer: Mick Easterby
Mick Easterby unleashed a very interesting prospect in Supreme Lad at Market Rasen's (LH : Soft) point to point fixture last January. Ridden by his son David, who put up fourteen pounds overweight (12st 7lb), the son of Supreme Leader was a most impressive twenty five lengths winner from Dry Hill Lad. The runner-up then went on to be beaten just seven and three quarter lengths by Extra Stout in the valuable Novices' Hunter Chase at Aintree on Grand National day. Having spoke to David Easterby during the Summer, the latest news is that Supreme Lad will go novice chasing and he is considered a better chasing prospect than his much hyped stablemate Noshinannikin.

POINTERS FROM IRELAND

The Irish point to point circuit is renowed for producing future stars and below are a select bunch of horses who made their mark 'between the flags' in Ireland last season. The majority have been purchased during the Summer by leading British trainers and should be followed this term.

BALLINLISS LAD (IRE) 6 ch g Bustomi - Sea Shrub
Trainer: N.T.CHANCE. Upper Lambourn, Berkshire.
Wins: (Apr 1998) 4/5yo Maiden at Taylorstown by 8 lengths (Good).
His victory came two seasons ago and, having joined Noel Chance last year, he picked up a leg injury and missed the whole term. He is OK now and is still held in the highest regard and he will go novice chasing in December. His victory at Taylorstown came at the expense of Prominent Profile.

BE MY MANAGER (IRE) 4 b g Be My Native (USA) - Fahy Quay
Trainer: Miss H.C.KNIGHT. Wantage, Oxon.
Wins: (Mar) 4yo Maiden at Athenry by 6 lengths (Heavy).
Previously trained by Tom Costello, he stands at 16.3hh.

BEST MATE (IRE) 4 b g Un Desperado (FR) - Katday
Trainer: Miss H.C.KNIGHT. Wantage, Oxon.
Wins: (Mar) 4yo Maiden at Belclare by 8 lengths (Soft).
Trained last season by Tom Costello.

BINDAREE (IRE) 5 ch g Roselier (FR) - Flowing Tide
Trainer: G.STEWART. Lisburn, Co.Down.
Wins: (Mar) 5/6yo Geldings Maiden at Loughbrickland by 10 lengths (Good).
Had earlier finished half a length second to subsequent Fairyhouse winner Southsea Native.

BRUTHUINNE (IRE) 4 ch g Vaquillo - Portane Miss
Trainer: Miss H.C.KNIGHT. Wantage, Oxon.
(Feb) Finished second in 4yo Maiden at Lismore (Soft), beaten 1 1/2 lengths. His name apparently means "house on fire."

CEANANNAS MOR (IRE) 5 b or br g Strong Gale - Game Sunset
Trainer: N.J.HENDERSON. Lambourn, Berkshire.
Wins: (Apr) 4/5yo Maiden at Summerhill by 25 lengths (Soft).
A full brother to Stormyfairweather, he was in the care of Enda Bolger last term.

CLASSIC ENIGMA (IRE) 5 ch g Classic Memory - Stoney Broke
Trainer: S.E.H.SHERWOOD. Lambourn, Berkshire.
Wins: (May) 5yo Maiden at Maralin by 15 lengths (Soft/Hvy).
He was very highly regarded by his former connections and it is likely he will go novice chasing.

COLONEL CHING (IRE) 5 b g Mazaad - Jamie's Lady
Trainer: C.J.MANN. Upper Lambourn, Berkshire.
Wins: (Mar) 5/6yo Geldings Maiden at Cloyne by 2 lengths (Good).
Trained last season by David Wachman, he has been bought by Stan Clarke during the Summer. His new trainer Charlie Mann describes him as "a lovely horse who will start off over hurdles."

COLQUHOUN (IRE) 5 b g Rakoposhi King - Red Rambler
Trainer: M.C.PIPE. Nicholashayne, Somerset.
Wins: (Jan) 5yo Maiden at Tyrella by 8 lengths (Soft to Heavy).
Subsequently finished second in a Down Royal (Good) bumper in May. Owned by Brian Kilpatrick, he was ridden on both occasions by Brian Hamilton and he rates him as "a serious prospect."

DAT MY HORSE (IRE) 5 b g All Haste - Toposki
Trainer: S.E.H.SHERWOOD. Lambourn, Berkshire.
Wins: (Apr) 5yo Maiden at Castletown-Geoghegan by a neck (Yld).
Regarded as "a serious prospect for the future", by his former trainer Denise Foster.

INCH ROSE (IRE) 5 b m Eurobus - Came To Believe
Trainer: N.T.CHANCE. Upper Lambourn, Berkshire.
Wins: (Jan) 5yo + Maiden at Lisgoold by 6 lengths; (Mar) 4yo + Winners of 3 at Bruff by 25 lengths (Soft to Heavy); (Apr) Gain Mares Final 4yo + at Ballynoe by a distance (Good).
Bought by Noel Chance during the Summer, she will reportedly go novice chasing.

IN YOUR INTEREST (IRE) 4 ch g Buckskin (FR) - Officer's Lady
Trainer: J.HALLEY. Ireland.
Wins: (Apr) 4yo Maiden at Kilmallock by 10 lengths (Soft to Heavy).

"He was bought at the Derby Sale and looks likely to be a very good horse," remarked John Halley after this good looking son of Buckskin had won readily.

MILLENNIUM WAY (IRE) 5 ch g Ikdam - Fine Drapes
Trainer: O.M.C.SHERWOOD. Upper Lambourn, Berkshire.
Wins: (Apr) Finished second in 4/5yo Mdn at Stradbally (Gd/Yld), beaten 2 lengths.

MURT'S MAN (IRE) 5 b g Be My Native (USA) - Autumn Queen
Trainer: P.F.NICHOLLS. Ditcheat, Somerset.
Wins: (Apr) 4/5yo Maiden at Tattersalls Farm by 3 lengths (Yielding).
Trained last season by Martin Treacy, he was bought at Goffs. He was held in the highest regard and has been purchased by John Hales during the Summer.

NATIVE CAPTION (IRE) 4 b g Be My Native (USA) - Hard Lady
Trainer: T.P.TATE. Tadcaster, North Yorkshire.
Wins: (Mar) 4yo Maiden at Lemonfield by 3/4 length (Heavy).
He was bought at the 1998 Land Rover Sales for Ir20,000gns by Enda Bolger. Described by Bolger as "a great lepper but still a big baby," he was bought by Tom Tate at the Doncaster Spring Sales in May for 56,000gns.

SEE MORE SENSE 5 b g Seymour Hicks - Flower of Tintern
Trainer: R.BARBER. Seaborough, Somerset.
Wins: (Mar) 5yo Maiden at Tallow by 20 lengths (Soft to Heavy).
Trained last season by Liam Burke, who stated: "He will make a lovely staying chaser in time. I'd imagine he will be running across the channel this season. He is one for the future." It is currently undecided whether he will be trained this season by Richard Barber or Paul Nicholls.

THE BUSHKEEPER (IRE) 5 b g Be My Native (USA) - Our Little Lamb
Trainer: O.M.C.SHERWOOD. Upper Lambourn, Berkshire.
Wins: (Apr) Second in 4/5yo Maiden at Tattersalls Farm (Yld), beaten 3 lengths.
Subsequently third in Naas bumper (Gd/Frm) in May.

SWITCHING STABLES

Below are a selection of horses which have switched stables during the Summer and look worth following for their new trainer.

CENKOS (FR) 5 ch g Nikos - Vencenza
Trainer: O.M.C.SHERWOOD. Upper Lambourn, Berkshire.
Oliver Sherwood takes charge of the ex-French gelding Cenkos from Kim Bailey. Unbeaten in

three hurdle races in France, he ran just once last term finishing fourth to Zafarabad at Newbury. A big lengthy gelding, he could make a very exciting novice chaser this season for his new connections.

FOREST ENDING (USA) 4 ch c Green Forest (USA) - Perlee (FR)
Trainer: J.A.B.OLD. Hackpen, Wiltshire.
"He is a lovely horse we bought last year. We have given him plenty of time and I am hoping he will make a nice hurdler this season," commented Jim Old about this ex-Henry Cecil trained four year old. Owner Wally Sturt went to 25,000gns at the Newmarket Autumn Sales for this Beverley maiden winner. A tall attractive son of Green Forest, he possesses plenty of scope.

MARTIAL EAGLE 3 b c Sadler's Wells (USA) - Twine
Trainer: C.J.MANN. Upper Lambourn, Berkshire.
Charlie Mann is particularly excited about the prospect of sending Martial Eagle novice hurdling this season. He was previously trained by Aidan O'Brien and he won a maiden at Cork (1m 6f : Gd/Fm) in June by a short head from Sahara Song. "He is by Sadler's Wells and is a half-brother to Alderbrook so you can't get much better than that. He is definitely one to follow," remarked Charlie Mann during the Summer. A fascinating prospect.

NATIVE SOCIETY (IRE) 6 b g Be My Native (USA) - Society News
Trainer: R.ROWE. Storrington, West Sussex.
Richard Rowe takes charge of the Nicholas Cooper owned Native Society. Bought for 30,000gns as a four year old, he made the perfect start to his career when winning a Wexford (Good) bumper by eight lengths two seasons ago, whilst in the care of Padge Berry. Native Society then ran three fine races over hurdles last term, twice filling the runners-up berth and finishing fourth on the other occasion. He did, in fact, look a certain winner on his latest start at Limerick (Sft/Hvy) only to be collared close home by Bramblehill Chief. However, that may prove a blessing in disguise as it means Native Society is still a novice over hurdles for this season.

SIR BOB (IRE) 7 b g Aristocracy - Wilden
Trainer: K.C.BAILEY. Northants.
"I can't wait to see him over fences next season," stated Billy McKeown after his exciting seven year old won for the third time last season at Carlisle in March. Unfortunately for McKeown, he was subsequently bought at the Doncaster Spring Sales for 78,000gns by Kim Bailey. He was purchased with the intention of going straight over fences this season and he should make a cracking novice. Sir Bob's other wins last term came at Newcastle and again at Carlisle. The key to this strapping son of Aristocracy, as far as a betting propositon is concerned, is stamina. He must have soft ground and he must have three miles as his former handler stated last term: "He needs three miles. Two and a half or even two and three quarters are no good to him." Three miles in soft ground at Towcester would appear his ideal conditions.

USK VALLEY (IRE) 4 b g Tenby - Penultimate (USA)
Trainer: P.R.CHAMINGS. Tadley, Hampshire.
Paul Chamings may not be a household name but when given the ammunition he is as good as the next trainer. He has a chance this season to really put himself on the training map with the potentially high class Usk Valley. He was held in the highest regard last season by Paul Webber and ran a super race to finish one and a half lengths second to Scarlet Emperor (Soft) in a

Kempton bumper in February. The fact the pair had pulled fifteen lengths clear of the third Captain Dee Cee (a winner since) confirms it was an excellent debut. He looks sure to win races.

THE FOREIGN LEGION

The following section nominates a number of horses to follow who have, up until this season, run abroad and are new recruits to the National Hunt game in Great Britain.

ADJIRAM (IRE) 3 b c Be My Guest - Adjriyna
Trainer: D.C.O'BRIEN. Tonbridge, Kent.
"He is a very exciting horse I bought privately off the Aga Khan in July," remarked under-rated young trainer Dan O'Brien about this ex-Alain de Royer-Dupre trained three year old. He certainly looks a fascinating prospect having won a Class B event at Longchamp this season. According to O'Brien, Adjiram will be gelded in November and his whole season will be geared towards the Glenlivet Hurdle at Aintree in April.

ARLAS (FR) 4 b g Northern Flagship (USA) -
Ribbon In Her Hair (USA)
Trainer: P.F.NICHOLLS. Ditcheat, Somerset.
The all conquering Paul Nicholls' team is further strengthened this season by the four year old Arlas. Trained in France by T.Civel, he won the Prix Ferdinand Dufaire at Auteuil (2m 5f : Holding) in May by a nose. The race was worth £53,821 to the winner. Arlas may well start the season over hurdles but expect to see him over fences in the New Year.

CARDIFF ARMS (NZ) 4 b g Lowell - Shuzohra
Trainer: Miss V.M.WILLIAMS. Kings Caple, Hereford.
Owned by *The Winning Line*, this ex-New Zealand trained horse is believed to be a most interesting recruit. A high class horse in his native country, he was narrowly beaten in their St Leger. He is currently in training with Mark Johnston on the Flat but he was bought with the main intention of going jumping and is expected to join Venetia Williams. A big strong horse, he is expected to go straight over fences and make use of the five pounds allowance his age group receives in novice chases.

HAPPY CHANGE (GER) 5 ch h Surumu (GER) - Happy Gini (USA)
Trainer: Miss V.M.WILLIAMS. Kings Caple, Hereford.
"Norman Williamson schooled him and was eulogistic. He said he is an absolute natural," reported Stephen Winstanley, head of *The Winning Line,* last season when the ex-German trained Happy Change was being prepared for the Champion Hurdle. Unfortunately, a slight training setback soon afterwards meant he has yet to race over the smaller obstacles but he looks a serious

prospect for this season. Third in the German Derby as a three year old, he has also won a Group 3 at Baden-Baden. Still eligible for novice hurdles, it is likely that his sights will be raised considerably higher this term. Watch out Istabraq !

KILLERINE (FR) 4 br g Leading Counsel (USA) - Rose Petal
Trainer: I.P.WILLIAMS. Alvechurch, Worcestershire.
Bought during the Summer, Killerine has tackled some of the best four year old hurdle races in France and, while he may go back there, he has been purchased with the main intention of going novice chasing in Britain. "He has Summered very well and has plenty of speed for the two mile novice chases," commented Ian Williams.

MAOUSSE HONOR (FR) 4 b f Hero's Honor - Maousse
Trainer: M.C.PIPE. Nicholashayne, Somerset.
Maousse Honor is already a winner this season having scored on her British debut at Worcester (Gd/Fm) in July by an effortless twelve lengths. She was bought at the Goffs (France) Mixed Sale earlier the same month for Ff480,000. Martin Pipe reported after her victory at the Midlands track: "She is a lovely big filly who will make a nice chaser one day." An easy winner at Auteuil in May, don't be surprised if she goes chasing after Christmas as she will receive a sex allowance as well as an age allowance. She looks sure to win more races.

MASTER HENRY (GER) 5 b g Mille Balles (FR) - Maribelle (GER)
Trainer: Miss V.M.WILLIAMS. Kings Caple, Hereford.
Despite being in training with Venetia Williams for most of last season, Master Henry has yet to see a British racecourse. A Listed winner on the Flat in Germany, he was recommended to The Winning Line by Graham Bradley. Significantly, the five year old did hold entries in the Cheltenham novice hurdles, at one stage, last term and had reportedly been impressing Norman Williamson immensely in his schooling. The latest news is that Master Henry may well bypass a hurdling career and go straight over fences. Whatever his connections decide, he looks a tremendous recruit to the jumping game.

The following horses were all bought at the Goffs (France) Mixed Sale at Saint-Cloud in July, and are all expected to race in Britain this Winter:

Bought by Hubert Barbe, who buys on behalf of Martin Pipe:
INTOX III 3 ch g Garde Royale - Naftane - Ff420,000
SWEET LAMBER 5 b g Mistigri - Sweet As Moss - Ff290,000
Bought by the BBA and are likely to be trained in Britain this season:
ALPENSTOCK 3 b g Mister Mat (FR) - Altaraza - Ff200,000
HELLO DE VAUXBUIN 4 b g Le Nain Jaune (FR) - Quadrille de Cuy - Ff190,000
IRIS D'ESTRUVAL 3 b c Quart De Vin - Claire d'Estruval - Ff320,000
ISARD III 3 gr g Royal Charter (FR) - Aurore d'Ex - Ff165,000

Bought by Noel Chance:
IRISH FASHION (USA) 4 ch g Nashwan (USA) - L'Irlandaise - Ff200,000
Twice a winner on the Flat as a two year old in France, he will be sent novice hurdling over two miles this season.

THE STARS AMONGST THE STORES

Below is a small selection of horses who have yet to see a racecourse but are held in the highest regard by their connections and are well worth noting this season.

CARDINAL SINN (IRE) 4 b g Mister Lord (USA) - Polly Glide
"He is a very nice horse who could well be aimed at the Festival bumper at Cheltenham." **MARK PITMAN**

HIGHLAND (IRE) 5 gr g Supreme Leader - Precipienne
"He is working nicely at home and is a grand prospect." **SIMON SHERWOOD**

KILCASH CASTLE (IRE) 5 b g Strong Gale - Cooleogan
"He is a very nice horse with a future." **AIDAN O'BRIEN**. Bought for Ir64,000gns at the 1998 Derby Sales, he is a half brother to Tullymurry Toff.

KING'S CRUSADER (IRE) 6 b g King's Ride - Fern Glen
"He's all class - a real big chasing type with bags of scope. He's a top class prospect." **FERDY MURPHY**

SPECIAL AGENDA (IRE) 5 b g Torus - Easter Blade
"We were going to run him at Newbury last season but he knocked himself beforehand. He works well at home and looks a very nice horse." **NOEL CHANCE**

TRIBAL LORD (IRE) 5 b g Supreme Leader - Pollyville
"He is a big strong chasing type and he has schooled very well at home. I have got high hopes for him." **IAN WILLIAMS**

CHARLIE MANN believes he has got "three very nice prospects for bumpers." "**BLUE RAIN** is a half brother to Decoupage and **LADY LUPIN** is a lovely filly and is a half sister to Lady Rebecca. **HISTORIC** is a son of Sadler's Wells but he failed to see a track when in training with William Haggas. He looks a lovely horse."

APPENDIX

Having entered the *Tote / Racing Post* Ten To Follow competition since its inception, it has given me both pleasure and frustration, but with the chance of winning over £200,000, plus monthly prizes, it is well worth a go, particularly as it is such a minimal outlay (£5).

To be amongst the leaders requires success in a number of the big bonus races such as the King George, Champion Hurdle and Gold Cup. This means that without prolific points scorer Istabraq in your line-up for the last two years your chances of being amongst the front runners would have diminished.

My favoured combination of horses is to include 5/6 chasers, 2/3 hurdlers with the big races in mind and also 2/3 novice chasers or hurdlers but always including a sprinkling of Irish horses as they tend to run more frequently and in races which are often not as competitive as English ones. One Jump Ahead is helpful for the competition (especially the novices) but obvious contenders such as Istabraq, See More Business etc. appear only in this Appendix. The following breakdown will hopefully prove helpful in selecting the type of horse necessary to do well in the competition.

TWO MILE CHASES
Paul Nicholls looks to have a very strong hand in this division. Reigning Champion **CALL EQUINAME** may well be stepped up in trip this term but his connections have the Queen Mother firmly in their sights later on. Stablemate **FLAGSHIP UBERALLES** may prove 'better value for money' as he is likely to run more often. He looked to be improving with every race last term. **DIRECT ROUTE** is a class act but he likes flat tracks and is more likely to win the Tingle Creek again than the Queen Mother. **EDREDON BLEU** is sure to win races again but possibly not at Headquarters. Tom Tate is still optimistic that **AGHAWADDA GOLD** can land a big prize this term.

KING GEORGE & CHELTENHAM GOLD CUP
It remains to be seen as to whether **TEETON MILL** makes a full recovery. **SEE MORE BUSINESS, FLORIDA PEARL, IMPERIAL CALL, DORAN'S PRIDE** and **LOOKS LIKE TROUBLE** are all likely to start off at Down Royal on 6th November. The latter, who won the Royal & Sun Alliance Chase, is likely to contest the Sean Graham Chase afterwards and then, all being well, the King George. **STRONG PROMISE** is reportedly back to full fitness and he heads to Wetherby for the Charlie Hall Chase (30th October). Ireland may well supply three interesting contenders in **RINCE RI, SIBERIAN GALE** and **SYDNEYTWOTHOUSAND** (See Irish Section).

CHAMPION HURDLE
As things stand, **ISTABRAQ** already looks unopposable for hurdling's Blue Riband. Of those who may develop into serious challengers, Mark Pitman believes **ASHLEY PARK** could go all the way and Jim Old believes we have still not seen the best of **SIR TALBOT** over hurdles. Norman Williamson was apparently very impressed when schooling the ex-German trained **HAPPY CHANGE** last season before a slight setback scuppered connection's plans. As so often is the case nowadays, many classy horses come off the Flat and make a successful transition to the hurdling ranks and develop into realistic Champion Hurdle contenders. That may well happen again this term.

STAYERS' HURDLE
At 40/1, **ANZUM** caused a shock in last year's renewal and the runner-up that day **LE COUDRAY** looks an obvious challenger again. Of the young pretenders, the nomadic **HORS LA LOI** may prove better over this longer trip than two miles, Paul Nicholls is to target his smart **NORSKI LAD** at this event and another juvenile from last year **KATARINO** may well emerge as a leading contender for this crown. A 'dark horse' for the race could be Mark Pitman's **JET TABS**. We have definitely still to see the best of him.

INDEX

SELECTED HORSE = BOLD *Talking Trainers = Italics*

ONE JUMP AHEAD UPDATES

For the fourth successive year, I shall be producing **3** mid-season *One Jump Ahead Updates*. Each *Update* comprises of information about the horses in *One Jump Ahead* (ie. their future plans or if they are injured), **New Stable Interviews** (last year's included **Ferdy Murphy** (February), which produced **15 winners** including **ARDRINA 14/1**, **Nicky Henderson** (March), including Cheltenham Festival winner **KATARINO 11/4** and **Henrietta Knight** (April), including **DICTUM 20/1** and **MIM-LOU-AND (9/1 & 3/1)**, **Regional Reports** (horses to follow from different areas of the country), **Point to Point News** (Hunter Chasers to follow), **Switching Stables** (news of any horses transferring yards), **Review of the Month** (analysis of a number of meetings from the previous month), **Big-Race Previews** and **News From Ireland**.

Last Season's *Updates*:

FEBRUARY
44 Winners including first time out winners **IN QUESTION (5/2), LADY CRICKET (4/1), BALLINCLAY KING (11/2), ASHLEY PARK (11/4), TOHUNGA (7/2)** plus **HEAD FOR THE HILLS (5/1), GREY EXPECTATIONS (7/2)** & **BUSHMAN'S RIVER (4/1)**.

CHELTENHAM FESTIVAL 1999
4 Winners: CASTLE MANE (9/2), BARTON (2/1), MAJADOU (7/4), ISTABRAQ (4/9) Plus: **Royal & Sun Alliance Novices' Hurdle:**
1st BARTON; 2nd ARTADOIN LAD (28/1) - Advised **EACH WAY Dual Forecast £92.20 (to a £1 stake).**

AINTREE GRAND NATIONAL Meeting
Winners: **MACGEORGE (11/1), DIRECT ROUTE (7/2), KING'S ROAD (3/1), KING OF THE CASTLE (7/2), EDELWEIS DU MOULIN (7/2)** Plus: **BLUE CHARM (2nd)** Advised **EACH WAY** at **66/1** for the **Martell Grand National.**

ONE JUMP AHEAD UPDATES
ORDER FORM

AVAILABLE AT £6.00 EACH OR £15 FOR 3
(Please Tick)

❑ **FEBRUARY 2000**
(Order to be received 27th JANUARY 2000)

❑ **MARCH 2000**
CHELTENHAM FESTIVAL PREVIEW
(This will be sent 1st Class on the Thursday before the Festival)

❑ **APRIL 2000**
AINTREE PREVIEW
(This will be sent 1st Class on the Friday before the Meeting)

❑ **OR   £15 FOR ALL 3**

Total Cheque / Postal Order value £............. made payable to M.H.PUBLICATIONS. Post your order to: M.H.PUBLICATIONS. 69 FAIRGARTH DRIVE, KIRKBY LONSDALE, CARNFORTH, LANCASHIRE. LA6 2FB.

NAME:...

ADDRESS: ....

.... POST CODE: ....

❑ Please tick if you are NOT interested in any of my FLAT PUBLICATIONS.